Contents

Executive summary: key findings and recommendations ii

Glossary of technical terms and acronyms vii

Introduction 1

1   Refugee realities: the view from the ground 7

2   The EU and asylum: growing influence, global reach 13

3   On EU territory: decisions about safety elsewhere 19

4   On the edges of the EU: 'managing migration' from Europe's neighbours 33

5   Regions of origin (I): new approaches to orderly entry 47

6   Regions of origin (II): enhancing protection or exporting asylum? 57

7   Countries of origin: the root causes of refugee flows 69

Summary of recommendations 88

Annex 1: Profile of Sri Lanka 94

Annex 2: Profile of The United Republic of Tanzania 99

Annex 3: Profile of The Democratic Republic of Congo (DRC) 104

Notes 109

Index 125

Executive summary: key findings and recommendations

The countries of the European Union (EU) host only a small and declining fraction of the world's 13 million refugees, but there are few more politicised issues than asylum in Europe. European policy makers have already introduced measures to limit and deter asylum seekers, but now asylum policy is being moved overseas. In the past two years alone, EU member states and institutions have presented an array of initiatives with one common theme: instead of receiving asylum seekers on EU territory, they propose to deal with them abroad.

All these proposals have real implications for the people who are fleeing for their own safety and often for their lives – implications which European governments have largely failed to consider.

This study measures the fast-moving 'internationalisation' of EU asylum policy against the very principles of refugee protection to which the EU has publicly re-affirmed its commitment. We trace asylum policy from EU territory to its borders and periphery, then from nearby transit countries to host countries in regions of origin, and finally to refugees' own countries.

The report draws together two strands of research. The first analyses the elements of EU policy that make up the internationalised asylum agenda. The second uses field research into refugee realities in Sri Lanka, the Democratic Republic of Congo (DRC), and Tanzania in order to bring hitherto silent voices into the EU's discussions.

On EU territory: decisions about safety elsewhere

All asylum seekers are entitled to have their claims individually examined in a full and fair procedure, regardless of their country of origin, their countries of transit, and their method of entry to the EU.

The 'harmonisation' of the divergent asylum laws of EU member states focuses on creating minimum standards for domestic systems, but contains two provisions with international implications. Asylum seekers from countries on so-called *'safe lists'* can be rejected without a full hearing. Our research in Sri Lanka demonstrated that no country can or should be designated as 'safe for all'. The prospect of rejection also confronts asylum seekers who have fled from countries where there are deemed to be *'non-state agents of protection'*. Even the military might of the EU's Operation Artemis in the Democratic Republic of Congo was only able to provide protection to a few people in a limited area. Both provisions make sweeping assumptions about conditions in countries of origin which could result in asylum seekers being returned to places where their lives and safety may be under threat.

Fulfilment of EU obligations to asylum seekers on their own territory must be the starting point for any global engagement. EU member states must eradicate subjective, selective, and outdated country-of-origin information from their decision-making processes. If states cannot base their domestic procedures on reliable information, there is little hope for the far more ambitious and complex extra-territorial plans.

On the edges of the EU: managing migration from Europe's neighbours

Controlling access: borders, barriers, and interception

Ninety per cent of asylum seekers are forced to enter the EU irregularly, because there are almost no channels through which they can obtain visas and travel documentation to enter regularly. The EU is investing a vast amount of money in efforts to prevent irregular entry. Measures include the deployment of border police, the placing of immigration liaison officers in foreign airports, the interception of migrants at sea, and penalties for air, rail, or road carriers who admit passengers without proper documentation.

These measures are subject to minimal scrutiny and accountability, because they are implemented outside state territory or 'privatised' by being delegated to airline and other carrier companies. The effect is to force asylum seekers to use dangerous channels of escape.

More than 5000 deaths of people trying to enter the EU have been documented – and many thousands more remain undocumented. Interception measures threaten the lives and safety of people seeking protection in Europe. EU member states must take responsibility for their actions and ensure that they do not have the effect of endangering people who are in need of protection. Immigration-control measures outside EU territory must include effective safeguards to ensure that claims for asylum are effectively assessed.

Securing the co-operation of transit countries

EU policy makers are seeking the co-operation of Europe's neighbours to 'manage migration'. Despite a commitment to development, this agenda dominates EU relations with key countries in North Africa and Eastern Europe. The European Neighbourhood Policy aims to share the benefits of the EU's 2004 enlargement with neighbouring countries, from Morocco to the Ukraine. But while improving refugee protection is not a priority, co-operation for migration management and control is.

Agreements on the readmission of asylum seekers, failed asylum seekers, and irregular migrants are also prioritised. These could in theory work positively: easing returns while providing a safety net to ensure that nobody is sent back to a place where his or her life or freedom may be in danger. However, in reality the practice is different: readmission agreements have been negotiated with countries such as China where the EU has expressed concerns about disregard for human rights, and with countries which have not signed the 1951 Convention Relating to the Status of Refugees, such as Syria. Our own research in Sri Lanka showed that the negotiation of a EU readmission agreement there has been premature, and few provisions are in place to monitor the consequences for returnees.

Farther afield: in refugees' regions of origin

Nearly all asylum seekers arrive in Europe 'spontaneously', of their own accord and often at considerable personal cost and risk. The EU's 'orderly entry' approach has explored ways to provide safe passage for a select number of refugees, direct from their regions of origin to the EU. Under this proposal, a resettlement scheme would select refugees from camps in regions of origin and grant them places in EU member states. This could offer a necessary lifeline to individual refugees who remain at risk and in limbo in camps. It would also be a gesture of willingness to share responsibility with host countries that are often poor and overburdened. Our research in the Congolese camps in western Tanzania revealed the need for any future scheme to be grounded in a full assessment of the needs and conditions in the target country, to ensure that selection is made according to need and vulnerability, and that resettlement is properly resourced so that it is not detrimental to the protection of those who stay behind.

Our research into the Swiss Protected Entry procedures in Sri Lanka demonstrates how a 'humanitarian visa' could also be an effective way of granting safe passage to a small number of vulnerable people who would be otherwise unable to access asylum, but similar proposals for an EU Protected Entry Procedure have received little political support.

These 'safe passage' measures need the same level of investment and political will as is currently afforded to the migration-management measures that prevent refugees from reaching Europe. These measures must not be employed at the expense of fair procedures for asylum seekers who succeed in making their own way to EU territory. They should be used to provide protection for selected vulnerable refugees, rather than as a strategy to control migration.

Enhancing protection or exporting asylum processing?

Since 2003, EU governments and institutions have explored ways of supporting refugees to remain in their regions of origin, so that they do not move on to EU countries.

Moving the processing of asylum claims to refugees' regions of transit or origin has been the most controversial element in the internationalised asylum agenda. Since the UK's proposal for Transit Processing Centres in 2003, this dangerous idea has been discredited on grounds of legality, morality, and practicality. It threatens to shift the responsibility for asylum processing to poorer countries outside the EU which cannot guarantee refugee protection. Nonetheless, the idea has re-emerged in the second phase of harmonisation and in initiatives proposed by Italy and Germany to establish centres in Libya and Tunisia respectively.

Other initiatives to improve 'Protection in the Regions' have the potential to make a more positive contribution to global refugee protection. Financial and technical assistance to refugee-hosting countries can help them to provide better legal, physical, and material protection to refugees. The proposals are presented both as a means of solidarity with the poor countries of first asylum that host more than 70 per cent of the world's refugees, and also as a means of migration management, reducing the numbers of secondary movements to the EU and creating the conditions for the return of asylum seekers from Europe.

However, key questions about resourcing and responsibility are unanswered, and the proposed division of responsibility between departments of home affairs and external relations is unclear. Programmes are expected to attain short-term migration-management goals, even though it is acknowledged that enormous investment over many years is required to make any significant difference to protracted refugee situations. Improving protection in the regions can only be achieved through long-term, well-resourced projects, implemented with the full co-operation and commitment of the countries in question and the full involvement of all stakeholders, including refugees themselves.

The true test of success is whether the measures taken result in an actual sense of security and well-being in a specific refugee context. Regional Protection Programmes must be based on thorough assessment of the real needs of refugees in actual situations.

Countries of origin: the root causes of refugee movements

The impact of external EU policy actions

Virtually all EU foreign policy actions – from human-rights monitoring, conflict management, development co-operation, and humanitarian assistance to arms-trade controls – have some direct or indirect bearing on the causes of refugee flight. Action to address root causes thus raises difficult questions of policy coherence or co-ordination between the divisions responsible for home affairs, development, and external relations. A lack of coherence can exacerbate the conditions that cause refugees to flee. As when the embargo on arms sales to Libya was removed in the interests of controlling migration, this home-affairs agenda is at odds with human rights and with humanitarian and development objectives.

Root causes demand serious engagement. Our research in DRC also revealed the difficulty of addressing the root causes of a complex conflict which has directly involved some six countries in the past eight years. EU action there is focused on holding together the peace. While action to reduce conflict and increase development assistance, humanitarian aid, and security may have longer-term impacts, the root causes of the conflict, such as its regional dimension and competition over minerals exploitation, have hardly been addressed by EU donors.

Coherence or co-operation? Joined-up EU policy

Although basic coherence between domestic and external policies on asylum and root causes has often been lacking, the EU's attempts to take joint action on the root causes of refugee flows and immigration have been largely ineffective, because of a lack of investment and consultation with the countries in question. They are marred by the domination of home-affairs concerns (to prevent irregular migration to the EU) rather than concerns for development, humanitarian assistance, or human rights. The need to address root causes has therefore slipped off the EU agenda, with the emphasis shifting from refugees' countries of origin to the countries of transit through which asylum seekers pass *en route* to the EU.

It is unrealistic and undesirable to expect policy makers whose experience relates to domestic asylum procedures and border controls to develop innovative projects for overseas development. Information sharing between policy areas must therefore be the guiding principle at all stages of project development, implementation, and evaluation. In addition to co-ordination within Brussels, it is important that EU policy makers incorporate the expertise of stakeholders in the countries in question, to assess need, guide implementation, and monitor impact of EU actions on root causes of refugee situations. In particular, the proposal made by the Commission in 1994, to see refugees themselves as a potential source of information on their countries of origin, should be revived.

The UNHCR in its Agenda for Protection called for a greater emphasis on addressing the root causes of refugee movement. EU leaders should heed this call.

The internationalisation of EU asylum measures should not proceed without guaranteed safeguards for refugee protection, based on a full understanding of refugee realities in countries of transit, first asylum, and origin. In particular, Oxfam GB calls for the following actions:

- EU member states must ensure fair and effective domestic asylum procedures in their own countries as a priority. International action must not be regarded as a substitute for this.
- EU institutions and member states must develop mechanisms to monitor their external actions and ensure that they respect international refugee-protection principles.
- EU institutions and member states must ensure that stakeholders are genuinely involved at all stages of design, implementation, and evaluation of extra-territorial measures, in order to ensure that these are responsive to real needs in specific refugee situations.
- The development units and foreign-affairs units of the EU and of member states must demonstrate leadership to ensure that home-affairs migration-management imperatives do not undermine or distort refugee-protection, humanitarian, development, and human-rights priorities.
- Host and transit countries engaging with the EU on asylum and migration-management initiatives must guarantee and demonstrate compliance with international refugee protection and human-rights law.
- European and international stakeholders, including NGOs and refugee communities and international organisations, must engage with the EU to ensure that policy is well informed by the realities of refugees' lives, and that implications for refugees are monitored. Given the broad implications of the new agenda, such stakeholders include development, human-rights, and humanitarian organisations.

Glossary of technical terms and acronyms

Technical terms

Asylum seeker: someone who has applied for asylum and is waiting for the authorities to determine whether or not he or she will be recognised as a refugee or given another form of protection.

Chapter VII mandate: Chapter VII of the UN Charter (article 42) provides that the UN Security Council may authorise the deployment of military forces in certain situations, for the purpose of restoring international peace and security.

Co-decision: a process for creating European laws, wherein the Council of the EU and the European Parliament 'co-decide' on a legislative proposal made by the European Commission. Unlike the 'consultation' process, where the Council may disregard the opinions of the Parliament if it chooses, in 'co-decision' the Parliament and the Council are equal legislative partners. Both institutions must accept a proposal in order for it to become binding law.

Convention refugee: a person who meets the specific legal definition of 'refugee' contained in the 1951 Convention Relating to the Status of Refugees (see 'Refugee' below).

Council of the European Union: formerly known as the Council of Ministers, this is the main legislative and decision-making body of the European Union. The Council represents member states' governments within the EU legislative process. It consists of ministers from each member state, but it may take different forms, depending on the subject to be discussed: i.e. each member state will be represented by the minister responsible for that subject area (external relations, justice and home affairs, transport, etc.). The presidency of the Council is held for six months by each member state on a rotating basis (although this system is subject to change under the Constitutional Treaty).

'Cross-pillar' approach: a way of developing EU policy whereby a specified objective (for example, promoting human rights abroad, or environmental protection) is pursued across multiple policy areas (for example trade, development co-operation, and defence).

Directives: legal instruments created by the institutions of the EU. They are binding on member states as to the result to be achieved, but decisions on the actual form and methods of achieving these results are left to individual member states. Directives must be transposed into national law by each member, within a specified time frame.

Durable Solutions: permanent solutions for refugees, the three Durable Solutions, as identified by UNHCR, are *local integration* (in a country of asylum), *resettlement* (to a third country), or *voluntary repatriation* (to the refugee's country of origin).

European Commission: an institution of the European Union, responsible for drafting proposals for new European laws, which it proposes to the Council of the EU and the European Parliament. The Commission consists of more than 24,000 civil servants, who must act independently of the governments of member states. It is responsible for ensuring that EU decisions are properly implemented, and for supervising the expenditure of EU funds. The Commission is divided into departments, known as 'Directorates General' (DGs), according to subject area (for example, DG Justice and Home Affairs).

European Community/European Union: the European Community (EC) forms the First 'Pillar' of the European Union (EU). The member states of the EU have agreed to pool their sovereignty and be legally bound by common European laws in certain matters (such as trade, economic and monetary union, development aid, and humanitarian assistance); these can be said to be 'Community matters'. The Council of the EU and the European Parliament together set the rules for activities in these areas. The Second and Third 'Pillars' comprise other policy areas, such as foreign / defence policy, where member states may seek common frameworks for action or adopt common positions, yet retain some degree of individual control (i.e. through the Council of the EU). These can be said to be 'EU matters'. Until 1997, asylum policies were contained within the Third 'Pillar'; from 2005, however, they have been transferred to the First 'Pillar'.

European Council: the term used to describe the regular meetings of heads of state / government of the EU member states. The European Council meets at least twice a year, with the objective of defining general policy guidelines.

European Parliament: consisting of 732 members (MEPs), elected directly by the people of individual member states, the European Parliament has the power to examine and adopt European legislation. MEPs do not sit in national blocs, but in seven political groups. The Parliament is charged with exercising democratic control, approving the EU budget, and assenting to international agreements concluded by the Union. The influence of the Parliament in making new European laws varies according to the subject area / legislative process (see 'co-decision', above). The Parliament has different committees to deal with particular issues (for example, foreign affairs, budgetary matters, etc.).

Harmonisation: the process by which EU member states are in negotiation to agree binding common standards to 'harmonise' their national asylum systems. The process began in 1999 with the Treaty of Amsterdam, which set out a five-year programme to create the first stage of the Common European Asylum System. Stage 2, set out in the Hague Programme, begins in 2005.

Internal flight alternative: a relatively new concept in refugee law, whereby recipient countries can argue that an asylum applicant need not be granted refugee status, because that person could find protection from persecution in another part of his or her home country, and therefore does not need to be granted protection abroad. This concept has been challenged by NGOs and also by UNHCR, all stressing that it should not be widely applied, and particularly not where it would be inhumane to expect the individual to relocate within his or her own country.

***Prima facie* refugee status:** refugee status accorded 'in the absence of evidence to the contrary'. This is usually granted in situations of mass influx, where individuals forming part of a certain group (ethnic or national, etc.) which is deemed to be particularly at risk are granted refugee status without an individual assessment being carried out.

Protracted refugee situation: a term used to describe a refugee situation where refugees have remained in isolated camp situations for extended periods without being provided with a 'Durable Solution' (see above). According to UNHCR, a protracted refugee situation is one in which refugees 'find themselves in a long-lasting and intractable state of limbo. Their lives may not be at risk, but their basic rights and essential economic, social and psychological needs remain unfulfilled.' Identifying such situations as ones where 25,000 or more persons have lived in exile for five or more years in developing countries, UNHCR has estimated that, at the end of 2003, there were 38 protracted refugee situations around the world.[1]

Qualified majority voting: the system of voting in the Council of the EU (in particular under the co-decision procedure, see above). This requires a decision to receive a set number of votes (each member state has a certain number of votes in the Council, weighted broadly on the basis of population), and is agreed by a majority of members. In addition, member states may also insist that the qualified majority represents 62 per cent of the EU's total population. If these conditions are not met, the decision will not be adopted.

Refoulement: refoulement occurs when a person is returned or transferred to a territory where his or her life or freedom may be in danger. 'Chain refoulement' describes a situation where an asylum seeker, transferred from the destination country (for example, in the EU) to a country through which he or she may have travelled (for example, in North Africa or Eastern Europe), is subsequently transferred again, from that transit country, back to a territory where his or her life or freedom will be in danger (usually, but not necessarily, the country of origin).

Refugee: according to the 1951 Refugee Convention, a refugee is someone who 'owing to a well-founded fear of being persecuted for reasons of race, religion, nationality, membership of a particular social group, or political opinion, is outside the country of his nationality, and is unable to or, owing to such fear, is unwilling to avail himself of the protection of that country...' (see 'Convention refugee' above). Other regional refugee instruments include a broader definition of a refugee which includes those who are fleeing widespread conflict or natural disasters.

Regulations: legal instruments created by the institutions of the EU which are directly binding on all member states. Their terms do not need to be transposed by individual member states into domestic law.

Acronyms

AENEAS	A programme established by the EU in 2004 for providing financial and technical assistance to third countries in the areas of migration and asylum
AFSJ	Area of Freedom Security and Justice
CEAS	Common European Asylum System
CFSP	Common Foreign and Security Policy
CoC	Code of Conduct
COI	Country of Origin
CSP	Country Strategy Paper
DDR	disarmament, demobilisation, and reintegration
DFID	Department for International Development (UK)
DG JHA	European Commission Directorate General for Justice and Home Affairs
DG Relex	European Commission Directorate General for External Relations
DRC	Democratic Republic of Congo
ECHO	European Community Humanitarian Office
ECHR	European Convention on Human Rights (1950)
ECSR	European Clearing System for Resettlement
EDF	European Development Fund
ENP	European Neighbourhood Policy
ERC	European Refugee Co-ordinator
ESDP	European Security and Defence Policy
EURASIL	European Union Network for Asylum Practitioners
FDLR	Forces Démocratiques de Libération du Rwanda
FLICT	Facilitating Local Initiatives for Conflict Transformation
GCIM	Global Commission on International Migration
HLWG	High Level Working Group on Asylum and Migration
ICARA	International Conference on Assistance to Refugees in Africa
ICC	International Criminal Court
ICMPD	International Centre for Migration Policy Development
ICRC	International Committee of the Red Cross
IDP	internally displaced person
ILO	Immigration Liaison Officer

IOM	International Organisation for Migration
IPKA	Indian Peace Keeping Force
JAI	Justice et Affaires intérieures
JHA	Justice and Home Affairs
JVA	Joint Voluntary Agency
LRRRD	linking relief, rehabilitation, and development
LTTE	Liberation Tigers of Tamil Eelam
MLC	Mouvement pour la Libération du Congo
MNF	multi-national intervention force
MONUC	United Nations Mission in the Democratic Republic of Congo
MSF	Médecins Sans Frontières
NRC	Norwegian Refugee Council
PEP	Protected Entry Procedure
RA	Readmission Agreement
RCD	Rassemblement Congolais pour la Démocratie
RPA	Regional Protection Area
RPP	Regional Protection Programme
RRM	Rapid Reaction Mechanism
RSD	Refugee Status Determination
SCIS	Source Country Information Systems–Sri Lanka
SCO	Safe Country of Origin
SEED	Small Enterprise Development
SIDA	Swedish International Development Co-operation Agency
SLMM	Sri Lanka Monitoring Mission
SPRAA	Special Programmes for Refugee-Affected Areas
TA	Treaty of Amsterdam
TPC	Transit Processing Centre
UNHCR	United Nations High Commissioner for Refugees
UNOCHA	United Nations Office for the Co-ordination of Humanitarian Affairs
UPI	Unit for Protection of Institutions
USAID	United States Agency for International Development
WFP	World Food Programme

Introduction

European asylum policy is being internationalised – moved overseas. In the past two years alone, policy makers in the EU member states and institutions have presented a diverse array of initiatives with one common theme: in response to the EU's obligation to receive asylum seekers *on EU territory*, they propose measures to deal with asylum seekers and potential asylum seekers *outside EU territory*.

These actions and proposals cover a broad spectrum of positive and negative interventions, each at a different stage of development or implementation. But individually and as a package, they all have implications for refugees' lives. This study maps the fast-moving 'internationalisation' of EU asylum policy in the context of the international principles of refugee protection – principles to which the EU has publicly affirmed its commitment.

The need for asylum is a symptom of the failure of protection.

Protecting refugees

The need for asylum is a symptom of the failure of protection. Seeking refuge is a vital last resort, a safety net for those who cannot find protection from abuses in their own country and so have to flee to find safety elsewhere. The rights of refugees to seek asylum and to be protected are set out in the 1951 Refugee Convention and in the full complement of international and regional refugee and human-rights instruments, including the European Convention on Human Rights.

These rights remain unfulfilled for many: from the 200,000[1] Sudanese refugees sheltering in harsh conditions in Chad, to the Afghan refugees in Pakistan, and the Somali refugees in Kenya who have remained in camps for decades without a solution, and the 150 Congolese refugees massacred in Gatumba camp in Burundi in August 2004. Violence, insecurity, and inadequate assistance are daily realities for many. The countries that host them may contain openly hostile elements, may erect barriers to prevent them from crossing their borders, or may simply be unable to cope with the impact of a large influx of destitute people.

Refugees' rights to protection are not always met in prosperous, stable countries either. In the countries of the EU, asylum policies and practice can result in hardship and violations of the rights of people seeking protection: they may be denied access to legal processes to claim asylum, or forcibly detained, or forced to return to places where their lives or safety are at risk.

Despite declining numbers of asylum seekers arriving in the EU, there are few more politically heated issues in Europe today than asylum. Developments across Europe, in countries that include Denmark, the Netherlands, Italy, the UK, and Ireland, have shown how public, political, and press hostility to asylum seekers fuels and has been fuelled by fears about race, security, and immigration in general.

At the same time, there is increasing co-operation between the member states of the EU to work together on asylum. Asylum has become an issue of increasing concern for the EU, and a central part of its Justice and Home Affairs agenda. EU member states are entering the second stage of harmonising their national asylum laws, having experienced in the first stage all the difficulties of co-operating on an issue which goes to heart of domestic politics and raises acute concerns about state sovereignty. Domestic asylum policies are at the core of this co-operation. The first stage of EU harmonisation set out minimum standards for national asylum systems: for the treatment of asylum seekers and the manner in which their claims should be decided. But parallel to this, and explicitly present on the agenda for the second stage, is an emerging preoccupation with international policies, or with externalising domestic responsibilities for asylum seekers.

This trend of 'internationalisation' includes actions and proposals to be implemented in the following contexts:

- around the *periphery of the EU*, to intercept asylum seekers before they reach the territory of member states;
- *in countries of transit*, to limit onward movement and process the claims of asylum seekers;
- in *refugees' regions of origin*, to increase protection capacity and establish 'orderly entry' mechanisms;
- and in *refugees' countries of origin*, to negotiate readmission and address the root causes of immigration and asylum seeking.

In the past two years, there has been an increased empasis on the 'international' or 'external' policy dimension. In the words of the former EU Commissioner for Justice and Home Affairs, 'the external dimension of asylum will grow in importance'.[2] While co-ordinated action on interception and the need to deal with root causes have been on the EU agenda for some time, there is a new concerted energy at the levels of individual member states, the collective European Union, and the international community, directed towards co-operation for international and comprehensive responses. In drafting the second stage of the EU Common European Asylum Policy, EU leaders have stated that 'asylum and migration are by their very nature international issues' and have called for the EU 'to continue the process of fully integrating migration into the EU's existing and future relations with third countries'.[3]

The proposals are not defined precisely, and the debate is developing rapidly, impelled by shifting political agendas, unilateral member-state initiatives, and reaction to incidents like the one involving African asylum seekers on the *Cap Anamur* ship in the Mediterranean (see Chapter 4). Each one of this array of actions and proposals is at a different stage of development and co-operation. For example, interception and readmission measures are in motion at EU, multilateral, and bilateral levels, but 'protection in the regions' is not, at the time of writing, far beyond the proposal stage.

In terms of refugee protection, some of the proposals, such as resettlement, are potentially positive in their effects; some, such as transit processing centres, threaten fundamental principles. Others, like regional protection programmes, remain too unspecific and raise too many basic questions for their implications for protection to be clear at this stage. Ultimately the potential for negative and positive impacts must be measured both against international principles and against the protection of individual refugees in specific situations – a consideration which tends to be missing from the equation when proposals are drawn up.

The internationalised agenda represents a movement of policy from DG Justice and Home Affairs (concerned with questions of how to operate an asylum system on home territory) into the realm of foreign or 'external' relations, humanitarian assistance, and development. Migration-management clauses are being integrated into EU external agreements with other countries; regional protection programmes include humanitarian assistance and development elements.

Reflecting this move, motivations behind the internationalisation of asylum are mixed. There is a recurrent stated commitment to improving protection for refugees in their regions of origin and in the countries through which they travel *en route* to the EU. But despite efforts to develop coherence and co-operation between the domestic and external policy areas, the agenda is predominantly driven by the central home-affairs agenda of 'managing migration' into the EU and controlling the numbers of asylum applications. This has resulted in 'international' asylum policies driven by domestic motivations and led by home affairs, often with little grounding in the realities of refugee situations. In the words of the UNHCR Director of International Protection: 'UNHCR is alarmed by the failure of the asylum debate in certain countries over recent times to properly reflect refugee realities on the ground – to properly take into account the problems of refugees, rather than only the refugee problem as such.' [4]

> *Every effort must be made to ensure that dialogue and co-operation are comprehensive, genuine, and meaningful.*

Consultation with stakeholders in the countries and regions in question is therefore essential. Governments and communities in refugee-hosting countries, refugees' representatives, international organisations, and NGOs all have valuable and detailed knowledge of 'refugee realities on the ground'. They are not only stakeholders who are and will be directly affected by internationalised asylum actions: they are also experts who can inform the development, implementation, and evaluation of the new plans, which extend far beyond the familiar territory and expertise of the home-affairs policy makers concerned with asylum seekers. Dialogue, partnership, and co-operation are familiar terms in the new proposals, but every effort must be made to ensure that dialogue and co-operation are comprehensive, genuine, and meaningful.

In October 2004, Oxfam GB organised a conference in Brussels, bringing together a range of stakeholders to begin a dialogue on the international dimension of EU asylum policy and to discuss ways of ensuring that refugee realities inform policy. Participants included refugees; government officials from EU countries and developing countries which host large numbers of refugees; policy makers from both the European Commission's home affairs and development directorates; representatives of international and European organisations concerned with refugees and migration; representatives of development, humanitarian, and asylum-focused NGOs; and independent experts from Europe and Africa. This report reflects many of the concerns and recommendations raised during those discussions.

Structure, method, and aims of this report

This study maps the elements of the EU internationalised asylum agenda and examines what they mean and could mean for protection of refugees in Europe and in the countries in question. Chapter by chapter, we trace the transfer of asylum policy overseas. We begin on EU territory, considering the elements of the domestic system that have international implications; we then move to the borders and peripheries of the EU; then to transit countries neighbouring the EU; then to host countries in refugees' regions of origin; and finally we address the question of EU action on 'root causes' in refugees' countries of origin.

Interwoven throughout the chapters are two strands of research and analysis: one presents the elements of EU policy that make up the internationalised asylum agenda, the other illustrates the refugee realities in countries and regions of origin.

For the first strand, desk research was conducted, in addition to extensive interviews in Brussels and The Hague (during the Dutch EU presidency) with EU policy makers, government officials, NGOs, international organisations, and independent experts.

The new internationalisation of EU asylum is moving fast; developments are constant and often difficult to track.

For the second strand, our researcher travelled to Sri Lanka, the Democratic Republic of Congo (DRC), and Tanzania to conduct interviews with refugees, internally displaced people (IDPs) and returnees, international and civil-society organisations, local and national government officials, and EU and European government delegations in the countries concerned. Key findings in response to each element of the internationalised asylum agenda are integrated in each chapter. Brief country profiles for each are included in the annexes; fuller versions will be available on the Oxfam website (www.oxfam.org.uk). These countries were selected because Sri Lanka and DRC have been significant as countries of origin of people seeking asylum in the EU; because all three countries have been the subject of external or home-affairs action or proposals which affect or will affect refugee protection; and because Oxfam GB has a well-established presence and a history of working directly with displaced people in each country.

Our analysis and recommendations are rooted in Oxfam GB's experience of working with displaced people and their host communities around the world, and in its work with refugees and asylum seekers in the UK. We are a rights-based organisation, working with others across the world to overcome poverty and suffering, and the internationalisation of EU asylum policy touches on many areas of our work, from humanitarian response in situations of conflict and displacement to development issues in refugees' countries of origin, refuge, and transit.

This study is intended as both a tool for reference and an agenda for action. The new internationalisation of EU asylum is moving fast; developments are constant and often difficult to track. This study aims to provide a clear introduction to the policies and issues at stake for those who are affected by, but often unfamiliar with, the internationalisation of EU asylum policy: policy makers in the fields of home affairs and external relations, and stakeholders, including refugees, government, and civil society, in the host and transit countries outside the EU that are the subject of proposals. The target readership also includes European and international and local NGOs, and international organisations working in humanitarian, development, and human-rights fields which have an important contribution to make in informing the development of EU proposals.

As an agenda, this study provides analysis and recommendations to ensure that the protection of refugees is not lost in the focus on 'migration management'. The internationalised asylum measures are moving beyond the areas of expertise of home-affairs policy makers, but they are driven by home-affairs concerns. It is necessary for policy makers in the EU and in member states to ensure that their internationalised asylum actions and proposals promote rather than undermine their commitments to refugee protection, as well as human rights, development, and humanitarian assistance.

Refugee protection is a global responsibility, but it is also very clear that the EU has direct and immediate responsibility for providing protection to refugees on its territory. Taking this as a starting point and using refugee protection and genuine dialogue as compass points, we argue that policy makers and stakeholders have the potential to shape EU policy to ensure that it has a positive impact on the lives of refugees in Europe and around the world.

Refugee realities: the view from the ground

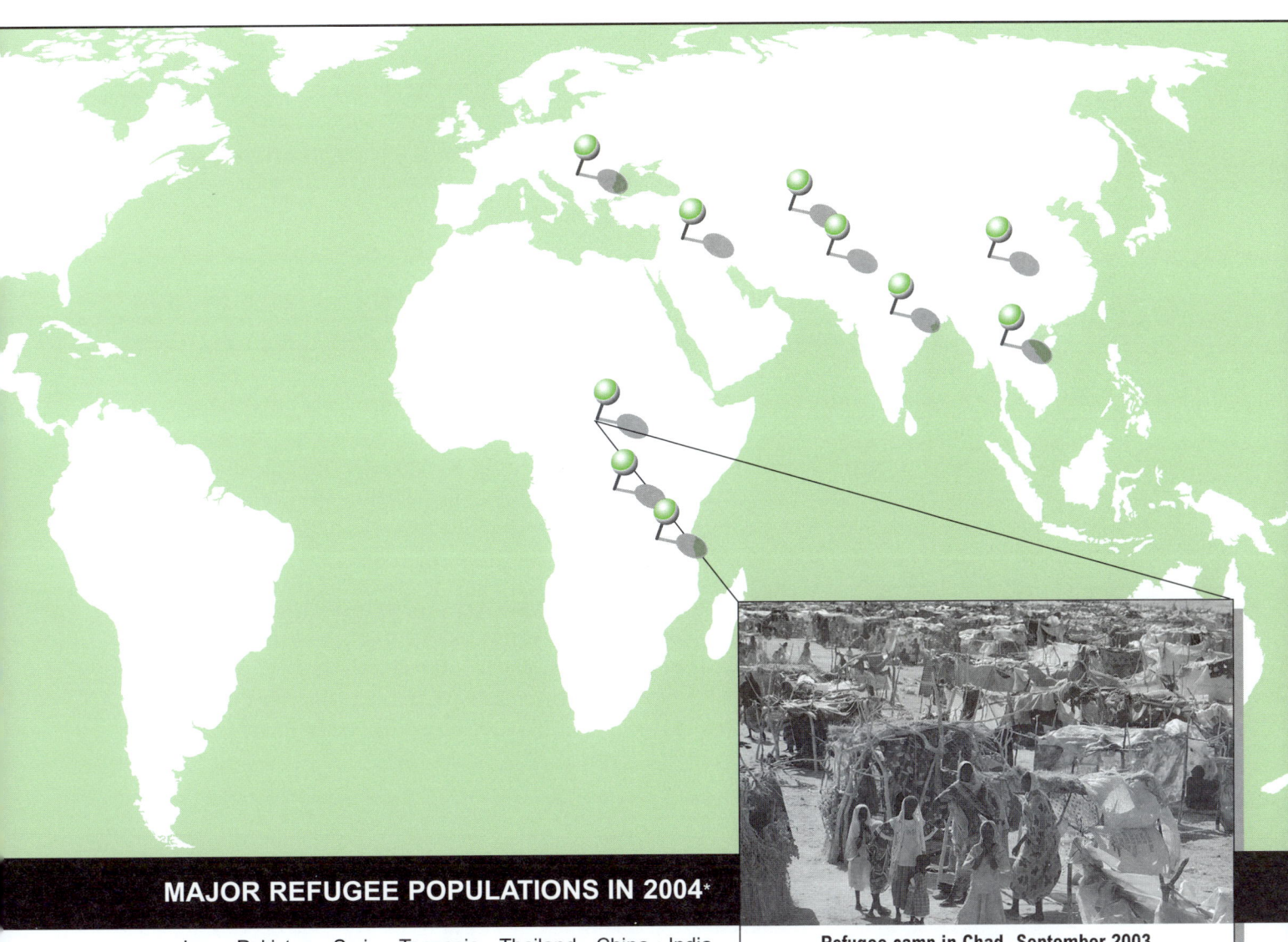

MAJOR REFUGEE POPULATIONS IN 2004*

Iran • Pakistan • Syria • Tanzania • Thailand • China • India
Serbia and Montenegro • Chad • Democratic Republic of Congo
(greatest first)

Refugee camp in Chad, September 2003
© Dieter Telemans

1
Refugee realities: the view from the ground

Across the world millions of people are forced to flee their homes. They are driven out by persecution for their political beliefs, targeted for ill treatment because of their ethnic group, or compelled to leave as a result of war or natural disaster. Some cross an international border and become refugees; others remain in their own country as internally displaced persons (IDPs). International law sets standards and locates responsibility for the welfare and protection of these people.

Developing countries produced 86 per cent of the world's refugees in the last 10 years, but also provided asylum to more than two-thirds of them.

Forced displacement: the size of the 'problem'

More than 13 million people are currently living as refugees.[1] This figure fluctuates as conflicts flare up and then recede, allowing people to return home.[2] In 1993, during the Balkan crises, the global refugee population peaked at 18.2 million.[3] Most remain near their countries of origin and live in poverty and insecurity. Ninety per cent of all UNHCR beneficiaries are hosted in developing countries in Africa, Asia, and the Middle East. These developing countries produced 86 per cent of the world's refugees in the last 10 years, but also provided asylum to more than two-thirds of them.[4] Since 1997, the Least Developed Countries (LDCs) alone have hosted about one quarter of the global refugee population.[5]

However, as vivid images of distress from Afghanistan to Sudan remind us, most people who uproot themselves to escape violence and deprivation, or who are forced to move by their government or other powerful groups, do not cross an international border. They become internally displaced people, few of whom wish, or indeed are able, to move farther afield. At the end of 2003, there were around 25 million IDPs, more than half (around 12.7 million) from countries in Africa.[6]

Daily threats

A large proportion of the world's refugees and IDPs remain displaced for extended periods of time. Despite a desire to return home, there is often no solution in sight to the violence and persecution that forced them to flee. Many, like the refugees in Kenya and in Pakistan, live in camps for decades. According to the US Committee for Refugees, 7.35 million refugees alone have been 'warehoused' in camps for at least ten years,[7] in forced dependency, often with inadequate assistance.[8] Denied the opportunity to earn a living or gain an education, and often with severely restricted freedom of movement, these people are deprived of their basic rights, as well as any possibility of planning a future or making a meaningful contribution to society.

Even basic security is often lacking in their new homes. Some camps[9] are the targets of attack. In eastern areas of the Democratic Republic of Congo (DRC), Oxfam spoke to people who had fled more than five times over the course of only one year because of frequent attacks on IDP camps. This situation is all too common. In Burma, Somalia, Indonesia, Sudan, and Chechnya, people move regularly to escape recurrent flare-ups of fighting. They receive limited humanitarian assistance: access is restricted by security conditions, or deliberately obstructed by the government or armed groups.

It is often the women, the elderly, the children, and the sick – people who experience discrimination even in normal circumstances – who are most at risk of deprivation and violence during conflict and displacement. In Ugandan settlements, camps in Darfur, and displaced communities in DRC, women and children have suffered widespread sexual violence. Girls frequently endure physical, psychological, and sexual abuse, in addition to heavy workloads both inside and outside the home. Forced labour and forced recruitment, often involving children, is a daily threat.

Outside camps, refugees face their own set of challenges. In countries with an 'encampment policy' that requires refugees to settle in designated camps, urban refugees exist in an illegal grey zone, without access to status determination, assistance, or protection. Human Rights Watch estimated that of the 60,000 refugees living in Nairobi in 2001, UNHCR recognised only 15,000 under its mandate.[10] In Dar es Salaam, Oxfam saw that such refugees are at constant risk of arrest and detention by local Tanzanian authorities and experience various forms of systematic legal, social, economic, and racial discrimination. Urban refugees around the world are exploited by employers and traffickers, and sometimes turn to prostitution or child labour in order to survive. Community-service organisations focused on the needs of urban refugees are rare, particularly when the general population itself is impoverished. Moreover, urban refugees often include multiple nationalities and ethnic groups, so that identification, outreach, and assistance delivery is much more challenging than in the contained setting of a camp. While some urban refugees are able to blend into their surroundings and support themselves, others are among the most desperate and vulnerable of all refugees.

In 1951, the United Nations adopted the Convention Relating to the Status of Refugees, the cornerstone of refugee law which sets out the basic rights of refugees.

Global standards to protect refugees

In 1951, the United Nations adopted the Convention Relating to the Status of Refugees, the cornerstone of refugee law which sets out the basic rights of refugees. These include access to education, employment, and health care, and freedom of thought and movement. Most importantly Article 33, concerning 'non-refoulement', prohibits the enforced return of a person to a territory where he or she may be exposed to threats to life or liberty. It defines a 'refugee' as someone who *'owing to a well-founded fear of being persecuted for reasons of race, religion, nationality, membership of a particular social group, or political opinion, is outside the country of his nationality, and is unable to or, owing to such fear, is unwilling to avail himself of the protection of that country'*.

This definition is complemented by the Cartagena Declaration, relating to Latin America, and the OAU Convention relating to Africa, both of which extend the definition of 'refugee' to cover people fleeing civil wars, ethnic violence, religious violence, and serious violations of human rights.

Refugees and displaced people, like everyone else, have human rights. Even in times of public emergency, States are never permitted to derogate from a core body of rights, which include the right to life, the prohibition on cruel, inhuman, or degrading treatment, the prohibition on slavery, and the prohibition on retroactive criminal laws.[11] The right to seek asylum is itself enshrined in the 1948 Universal Declaration of Human Rights. In times of conflict, refugees and displaced people can be protected as civilians under International Humanitarian Law.

Who is responsible for protecting refugees?

States have the primary responsibility to protect all people on their territory. For refugees this includes providing fair and accessible asylum procedures, ensuring that their basic needs are met, and helping people to find durable solutions. However, particularly in situations of mass influx of refugees, host countries may lack the capacity and resources to protect refugees and they may therefore require international assistance. The principle of international solidarity to assist, protect, and find solutions for refugees has been affirmed in a declaration signed in 2001 by states parties to the 1951 Convention. It declares that 'respect by States for their protection responsibilities towards refugees is strengthened by international solidarity involving all members of the international community and that the refugee protection regime is enhanced through committed international cooperation in a spirit of solidarity and effective responsibility and burden-sharing among all States'.[12]

The right to seek asylum is itself enshrined in the 1948 Universal Declaration of Human Rights.

State assistance is often channelled through the Office of the United Nations High Commissioner for Refugees (UNHCR), which was created in 1950. It is mandated to lead and co-ordinate international action to protect refugees and resolve refugee problems worldwide. Its primary purpose is to safeguard the rights and well-being of refugees. It strives to ensure that everyone can exercise the right to seek asylum and find safe refuge in another State, and find a permanent solution to their displacement. In addition to providing and co-ordinating basic assistance, UNHCR works to ensure access to basic refugee-determination procedures and the granting of basic rights, without discrimination, consistent with international law. On request by the Secretary General or the General Assembly and with consent of the state concerned, UNHCR's mandate sometimes covers internally displaced persons as well. This is the case, for example, in Sri Lanka.

However, large numbers of other organisations also work on a daily basis with refugees, including UN agencies such as the World Food Programme (WFP), which provides food aid; the treaty-based International Organisation for Migration (IOM), which provides transportation; and international and national NGOs, which often provide the majority of basic services – from water and health care to education and legal representation.

The daily contact between refugees and the staff of these NGOs has led to a recognition that, in order to address the critical threats to people's health, lives, livelihoods, and security, the provision of material assistance alone is inadequate. In response, some NGOs are working to improve the protection of refugees by identifying the threats and acting to influence, support, and sometimes substitute for the responsible authorities who are failing to protect them. Community-empowerment strategies are essential to reinforce people's protection, their coping mechanisms, and their ability to advocate on their own behalf: 'wherever access and contact permit, humanitarian protection work is ... about working directly with protected persons to identify and develop ways that they can protect themselves and realize their rights to assistance, repair recovery, safety and redress'.[13] Populations at risk know most about their own resources, their situations, and the motivations of those who threaten them.

Ending displacement: Durable Solutions

Finding a durable solution is the only way to guarantee displaced people a life of dignity and security, with the fulfilment of all their rights. UNHCR sets out three durable solutions for refugees: *local integration, resettlement to another country,* and, in most cases, *voluntary repatriation*.

Local integration is an alternative to the 'warehousing' of refugees. It allows refugees to pursue an independent livelihood. It is a legal and social process, conferring a wider range of rights and entitlements in the host state, which may ultimately lead to the granting of citizenship. While there are successful examples of integration in countries such as Pakistan, and in Tanzania under President Nyerere, many countries or host populations in developing or least-developed countries are unwilling to pursue local integration, fearing depletion of resources and creation of insecurity or resentment among the local communities.

Resettlement to a third country is another option. It is a targeted mechanism which allows refugees in camps to be selected and transferred to another country to start a new life. It is used to facilitate family reunification; to meet the needs of specific vulnerable groups such as survivors of torture; or as a protection intervention where a refugee's security is at risk in the refugee camp. The resettlement of thousands of Somali Bantu from camps in Kenya to the USA is an example of large-scale refugee resettlement. In other cases individuals are selected according to a quota system. However, the number of people resettled each year is tiny: only 28,255 in 2003, according to UNHCR – about 0.2 per cent of the global refugee population.

This leaves the third alternative: helping people to return home to rebuild their lives. It is the most desirable option for many refugees and IDPs, but it is often a sensitive and difficult process, with people returning to destroyed or occupied homes, where they lack the basic essentials for survival and they are subject to continuing tensions and harassment.

To be effective, repatriation must mean 'voluntary return in safety and dignity'.[14] The 'push factors' in the place of temporary refuge should not exceed the 'pull factors' in the country of origin. In practice, many refugees feel compelled to return home prematurely because assistance in a camp or settlement has been reduced, or protection is inadequate. According to UNHCR, the concept of dignity means that returning displaced families are 'not manhandled, that they can return unconditionally and if they are doing so spontaneously they can do so at their own pace, that they are not arbitrarily separated from family members; and that they are treated with respect by the authorities and full acceptance by the national authorities, including the full restoration of their rights'.

Respect for the dignity of refugees must be central to the way in which they are treated, not only during repatriation, but at all stages of their flight and search for solutions. Host states, whether in developing countries, or rich Western countries of asylum, as well as international and national agencies and host communities, have a responsibility not to reduce the human rights of displaced individuals to basic survival or the letter of the law or a minimal interpretation of it.

The EU and asylum: growing influence, global reach 2

COUNTRIES OF ORIGIN OF INDIVIDUALS SEEKING ASYLUM IN EUROPE – TOP 10*

Russian Federation • Serbia and Montenegro • Turkey • China • Nigeria
India • Algeria • Pakistan • Democratic Republic of Congo • Georgia

(greatest first)

Asylum-seeker child at Red Cross centre, Sangatte, France 2001
© H.Davies/Exile Images

2
The EU and asylum: growing influence, global reach

> *It would be in contradiction with Europe's traditions to deny [the freedom that Union citizens take for granted] to those whose circumstances lead them justifiably to seek access to our territory. [...]Common policies [on asylum and immigration] must be based on principles which are both clear to our own citizens and also offer guarantees to those who seek protection in or access to the European Union.*
> Conclusions of Tampere European Council, October 1999[1]
>
> *82% of those questioned thought the government's policies on immigration and people who sought asylum in Britain were 'not tough enough'. [...] Some 80% of those polled agreed with the statement that 'the problem of asylum seekers is out of control'.*
> 'Asylum problem "out of control"', *Daily Mail* (UK), 18 August 2003

EU and asylum policy: a collective concern

The countries of the EU, like all others, are faced with people wishing to enter from many backgrounds, for many reasons, and for varying durations. They include short-term visitors for tourism, personal reasons, or business reasons, and temporary or longer-term migrants arriving to work or join their families. They also include people seeking safety or 'asylum' from persecution elsewhere.

The member states of the EU have obligations towards these asylum seekers under the 1951 Convention as well as under the European Convention of Human Rights and other human-rights instruments, They have publicly reaffirmed their commitment to these responsibilities, although in practice they have often fallen short of meeting them. The threat of terrorism, the enlargement of the EU, and the 'mixed' flows of refugees and other migrants all pose challenges. But, as Human Rights Watch notes, 'European governments and institutions did not rise to these challenges, instead continuing to scale back rights protections – in particular for asylum seekers and migrants'.[2]

While member states are responsible for asylum seekers on their territory, over the past decade EU institutions have gradually assumed more responsibility for co-ordinating immigration and asylum policy. This process has 'harmonised' the basic elements of member states' asylum policies and has also introduced a new international element. Such co-operation has not been easy, a fact which has often resulted in low standards of refugee protection. Asylum is an issue of concern for the EU, because the EU is an area of free movement. Collective agreement on free migration *between* EU member states means collective regulation of limited migration *into* EU member states.

The European Community was established as a common area where member states could freely move and trade their goods, an initiative which entailed the need for the free movement of people within this area. In turn, the free movement of persons within the European Community required co-ordinated control of its external borders: that is, control over who would be allowed to enter this area of free movement. Co-ordinated control over external borders entails the co-ordination of European states' policies on immigration and, of course, on asylum. So, since the early 1990s, the member states of the European Union have co-operated on issues of asylum and immigration, as well as borders and frontiers.

But in an age of globalisation and of fears about common security, immigration goes to the very heart of a state's sovereignty. This creates a tension. On the one hand, EU member states acknowledge that they need to co-ordinate control of their borders. Such co-ordination requires states to make compromises if their national laws differ. On the other hand, the political reality is that states wish to retain as much control of these policies as possible: to decide, simply, who may and may not enter, and remain in, their territory, and under what conditions.

Early measures to co-ordinate immigration and asylum policies gave the European Union institutions little power, and they tended to be non-binding. This method of co-ordination proved unsatisfactory. There was a lack of transparency, and a general lack of co-ordination between different bodies working on the same policy areas.

A greater role for the EU

With the rise in the number of asylum applications made within the EU during the 1990s, there was increasing political will to agree a common EU approach to asylum. EU member states felt that co-ordinated action was primarily necessary to increase the efficiency of border controls. Increasing media attention, claims that some member states had 'softer' asylum policies than others, and perceptions of widespread 'asylum shopping' to take advantage of the different provisions in each country prompted calls for a harmonisation of asylum laws across member states.

The result was the Treaty of Amsterdam (TA) in 1997, which reshaped co-operation on Justice and Home Affairs (JHA) issues and affected EU asylum policy in two ways. Firstly, it set an agenda for harmonisation of asylum policies throughout the EU. Secondly, it changed the way in which policy is actually developed by the institutions of the EU. In setting an agenda for harmonisation, the Treaty of Amsterdam identified the basic building blocks of a common EU asylum system, and set 2004 as the deadline for these elements to be agreed by all member states and adopted as EU law.

The results of this harmonisation have been disappointing. Overall, political considerations, combined with the difficulties of making unanimous policy, have resulted in 'lowest common denominator' standards in the asylum instruments adopted by the EU since 1999.

Political considerations have resulted in 'lowest common denominator' standards in the asylum instruments adopted by the EU since 1999.

The standards finally agreed are often set at a level below domestic standards in many member states; indeed, they sometimes fall below the minimum standards required by international law.[3]

The way in which these 'minimum standards' have been agreed reveals a further tension within EU policy making on asylum. On the one hand, numerous EU declarations affirm the importance of upholding human rights through the actions of the EU and its member states. At the October 1999 European Council in Tampere, Finland, for example, EU heads of government stated their intention to develop 'an open and secure European Union, fully committed to the obligations of the Geneva Refugee Convention and other relevant human rights instruments, and able to respond to humanitarian needs on the basis of solidarity'. The same conclusions also reaffirmed 'the importance the Union and Member States attach to absolute respect of the right to seek asylum'.[4]

On the other hand, member states' actions, both in negotiating EU legislation, and in taking unilateral measures, have repeatedly shown that the overriding concern of member states is to reduce the numbers of asylum seekers on their territory. This is seen in the emphasis placed on increasing border controls (to limit access to asylum procedures), and on limiting the rights of those who do manage to lodge an asylum claim within the EU. Such measures are difficult to reconcile with the stated concern for upholding human rights in general, and the right to seek asylum in particular.

A new international dimension for asylum

In addition to its efforts to harmonise policies within Europe, the EU sought a more international approach to immigration and asylum. At the Tampere European Council, EU leaders called for 'a comprehensive approach to migration addressing political, human rights and development issues in countries and regions of origin and transit'. They invited member states and the Union to contribute to 'a greater coherence of internal and external policies of the Union'.[5]

The focus shifted to partnerships with third countries in regions of origin and transit. The EU's asylum-related policies would not concentrate exclusively on the situation within the EU (i.e. within the 'area of freedom, security and justice'), but now would also try to influence regions bordering the EU, and / or in asylum seekers' regions of origin. Increasing priority is given to this agenda. The 'Multi-annual Strategic Programme', prepared by the EU Presidencies for 2004–6 (Ireland, Netherlands, Luxembourg, UK, Austria, and Finland), stated that 'the continued integration of the Justice and Home Affairs into the Union's external policies and a deepening of that process will remain a key feature of the programme in the period from 2004'.[6]

The growing importance of this 'external dimension' is apparent in the plethora of recent proposals made by the Commission and by individual member states. These will be examined in detail in the chapters that follow.

A new way of making EU asylum policy: room for consultation?

The Treaty of Amsterdam gave the institutions of the EU (the European Commission, the European Parliament, and the Council of the European Union) more power in making asylum policies which would be legally binding on member states. It also defined the various roles that the European institutions will play in this process, and the 'balance of power' between them.

After a transition period, the European Parliament would have more say in decision making on asylum matters: there would be a greater degree of oversight by the democratically elected Members of the European Parliament (MEPs). From 2005, the Council of the EU (consisting of ministers from member states' governments) will 'co-decide' with the Parliament on proposals put forward by the Commission (the body that proposes and implements legislation). Decisions in the Council will be made on the basis of qualified majority voting. In practice, this means the removal of individual member states' veto on asylum legislation.

Learning from refugee realities?

The decisions made by the EU institutions on asylum are determined by the interests and priorities of the EU's member states. From now on, they are also subject to the democratic scrutiny of the elected members of the European Parliament, and the legal scrutiny of the European Court of Justice. But how does the EU ensure that its asylum policies accord with global standards to protect refugees? In addition, where its policies concern the 'external dimension,' how can the EU ensure that its decisions are informed by realities in the countries with which they are dealing?

How does the EU ensure that its asylum policies accord with global standards to protect refugees?

The policy makers who are developing this 'internationalised asylum agenda' are based in Brussels or in the capitals of member states, and they have a focus on Home Affairs (the portfolio in which asylum and migration are mostly dealt with). In the absence of direct experience or expertise in international issues of refugee protection, it is imperative that policy makers should consult with individuals and organisations which have such knowledge and experience.

There is a need for greater internal consultation with colleagues in foreign-affairs and development ministries or directorates. As this study shows, attempts at such 'joined-up' policy making have been limited to date, and have resulted in conflicts of interest and dominance by the home-affairs agenda. There is also a need for external consultation with the international organisations and non-government, civil-society, and refugee groups whose direct and current experience of the realities of refugee situations should be a vital resource for policy makers. A declaration annexed to the Treaty of Amsterdam states that 'consultation shall be established with the United Nations High Commissioner for Refugees and other relevant international organisations on matters relating to asylum policy'.[7] The call has been repeated by the European Council [8] and by the Parliament.[9] Whether or not it has been heeded and has succeeded in closing the 'refugee reality gap' will be seen in the following chapters.

On EU territory: decisions about safety elsewhere   3

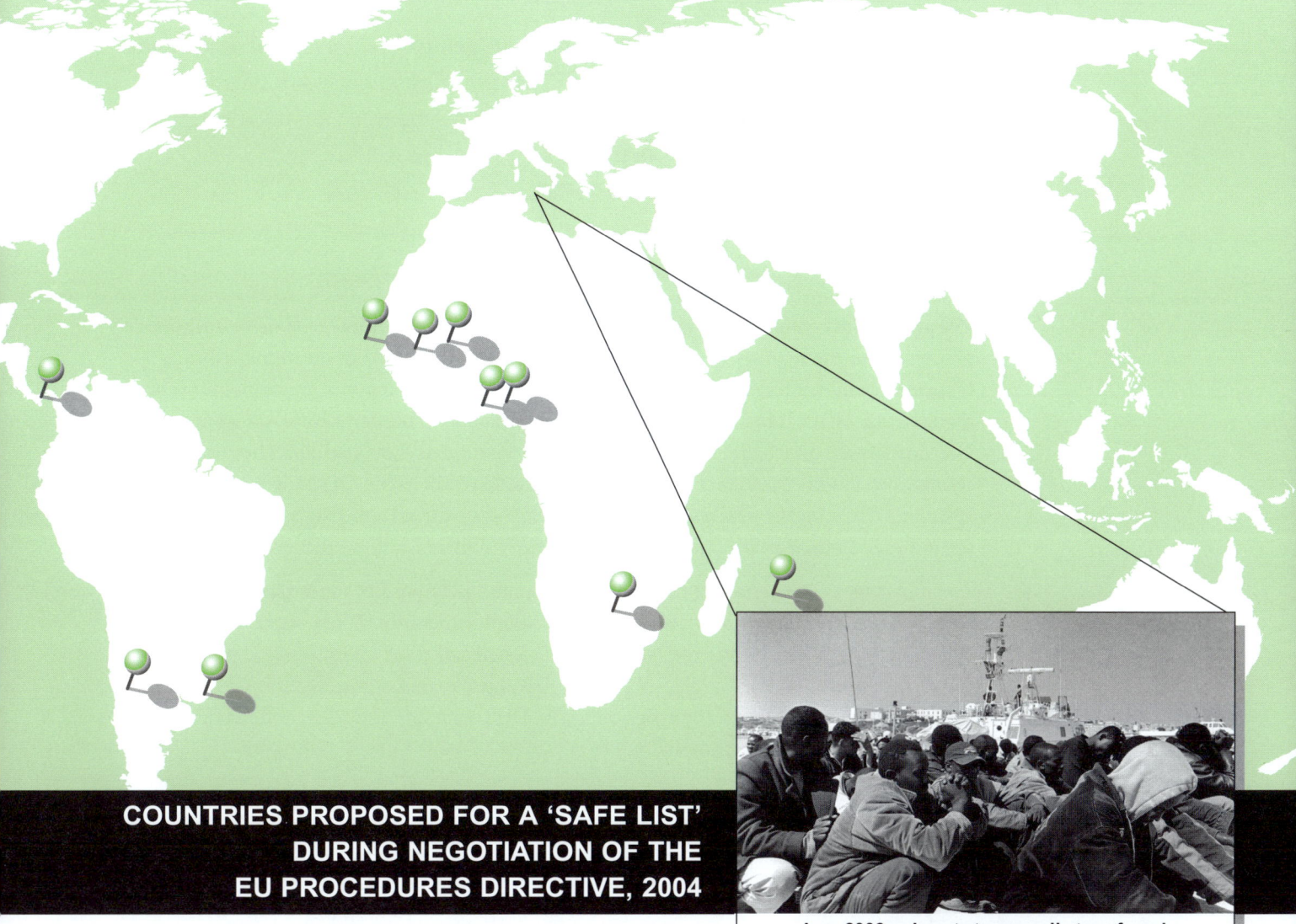

COUNTRIES PROPOSED FOR A 'SAFE LIST' DURING NEGOTIATION OF THE EU PROCEDURES DIRECTIVE, 2004

Benin • Botswana • Cape Verde • Chile • Costa Rica
Ghana • Mali • Mauritius • Senegal • Uruguay

June 2003: migrants temporarily transferred to a centre on the Italian island of Lampedusa, after landing on the Sicilian coast

© Francesco Cocco

3
On EU territory: decisions about safety elsewhere

> *'Everyone pays lip-service to the notion that "genuine refugees need and deserve protection" – this is the raison d'être of the international asylum system. The reality, I'm afraid, is that Europe's asylum systems do not always afford refugees the chance to state their claim.'*
> Ruud Lubbers, UN High Commissioner for Refugees, 5 November 2004[1]

Harmonising asylum policy: an opportunity missed

The agreed instruments which harmonise EU asylum policy [2] focus on *domestic* asylum processes, i.e. the manner in which people are treated on EU territory. Although the instruments may indirectly influence the willingness of other regions or countries to adopt high standards, most have limited direct impact beyond EU borders. However, some of these instruments are directly relevant to the 'internationalised asylum agenda'. They make bold claims about safety in other countries and they could result in moving people to dangerous situations. This chapter will therefore examine two issues: that of non-state agents of protection in the Refugee Definition Directive, and that of 'safe countries' in the Procedures Directive.

The first stage of harmonising the asylum laws of the EU member states has recently reached an unsatisfactory conclusion after five years of lengthy and difficult negotiations. The process began in 1999, when the Tampere European Council called for a common EU policy on asylum and immigration, comprising a Common European Asylum System (CEAS), partnerships with refugees' countries of origin, fair treatment of foreign nationals, and the management of migration flows.[3]

The CEAS consisted of two stages. The first was the creation of five legal 'building blocks', a set of instruments mostly setting minimum standards to harmonise the basic elements of member states' asylum policies.[4] Once these had been agreed at the EU level, states would have two years to transpose these 'minimum standards' instruments into their national laws. The second stage of the CEAS began when the building blocks had been agreed. In November 2004, the European Council adopted 'The Hague Programme', outlining a five-year agenda for increased co-operation on EU asylum and immigration policy. The Council emphasised the importance of transparency and the involvement of the European Parliament, and called on the Commission to present an Action Plan in 2005. It has also stated that the elements of this plan should be based on 'the full and inclusive application of the Geneva Convention on Refugees and other relevant treaties'.[5] Similar promises made at Tampere in 1999 have largely remained unfulfilled.

The primary aim of the CEAS was to create consistent conditions across the EU, in response to the problems caused by the major divergences in member states' national asylum laws. These differences meant that, for example, an asylum seeker persecuted by rebel groups in Algeria would be granted refugee status in the UK, but not in France. The problems posed by this 'protection lottery' had to be addressed. Governments also wanted to make sure that their treatment of asylum seekers was on a par with their neighbours', because they were fearful of 'asylum shopping'. A harmonised system offered an opportunity to put an end to the common tendency for states to amend their national legislation to ensure that it was not 'softer' than that of their neighbours.

The CEAS gave EU decision makers an opportunity to adopt examples of good practice and ensure high standards in asylum systems, in line with their recent public commitment to the 1951 Refugee Convention. With the exception of some positive provisions, this potential was not realised. The harmonisation process has instead resulted in EU instruments which conform to the lowest common denominator. While they ought not to require member states to bring their domestic law down to this 'minimum' level, the instruments adopted give them the latitude to lower their standards. Member states may fear that if they fail to bring their standards down to the level of their neighbours, their share of asylum seekers will increase. As one expert has noted, this 'domino effect' could mean widespread 'harmonising down', leading to a worrying situation whereby 'standards which have been presented as a minimum would instead become the norm'.[6]

Although the political imperatives of member states were largely responsible for the low standards, a contributing factor has been inadequate consultation with external experts and stakeholders. While Commission staff have suggested that formal mechanisms are unnecessary with regard to asylum (as there is a small group of stakeholders), stakeholders believe that the methods of consultation are still unstructured and devised on an *ad hoc* basis. Stakeholder groups generally agree that the Commission does receive input from NGOs and UNHCR, yet the lack of formal structures means that many NGOs are excluded from the consultation process. Refugee groups are entirely missing. At the same time, the Council of the EU rarely asks stakeholders for their input, and there has been a general lack of transparency.

The lack of formal structures means that many NGOs are excluded from the consultation process. Refugee groups are entirely missing.

In line with the Treaties of Amsterdam and Nice, the role of the European Parliament in policy making on asylum will increase from 2005.[7] This could be important, because the Parliament has tended to maintain more meaningful dialogue with stakeholder groups on asylum and immigration matters. The Parliament could also play a crucial role in assessing the legality of certain instruments before the European Court of Justice (a role whose usefulness has already been demonstrated with regard to a Directive on Family Reunification).[8]

The Refugee Definition Directive

The Refugee Definition Directive[9] provides a common EU definition of who is a refugee, and/or who is otherwise in need of international protection ('subsidiary protection' status for those who do not fit the strict Convention definition but who have a right under the provisions of European and international human-rights law not to be returned and to be given protection).

The Directive also defines the rights of those who are granted either status. It aims to end the existing 'protection lottery' by ensuring that EU member states interpret their obligations consistently.

The Directive's definition of a refugee largely follows that of the 1951 Convention. There are some positive features: the Directive accounts for both 'Convention' refugees and also other persons in need of international protection. Gender-specific persecution is explicitly recognised in this Directive, which means that a female asylum seeker with a well-founded fear of, for example, sexual violence, forced marriage, female genital mutilation, forced prostitution, or punishment for transgressing repressive social customs will now be entitled to refugee status across the EU.[10]

Crucially, non-state actors are now recognised as possible agents of persecution; so, in the example above, the Algerian asylum seeker would now be eligible for refugee status in any member state.

However, the Directive also includes a worrying reference to non-state agents of *protection*. The Directive regards parties or organisations (including international organisations) which are 'controlling the State or a substantial part of the territory of the State' as potential sources of protection against persecution.[11] A member state can reject an asylum claim on the grounds that it believes that a 'non-state agent of protection' exists in the asylum seeker's country of origin. The fundamental instruments of international refugee law do not contain any such reference. Despite this, some member states have already rejected numerous asylum claims by Kurds from northern Iraq, on the basis that these people could get protection from authorities in the Kurdish Autonomous Area (KAA). In 2002, however, the UK Court of Appeal ruled against this practice, stating that the KAA could not be considered like a state, and could not guarantee protection for the purposes of the Refugee Convention. The Qualification Directive could allow member states to ignore such jurisprudence, putting people in danger by sending them back into the hands of 'non-state agents of protection' who cannot actually guarantee their safety.

Some member states have rejected claims by Somali asylum seekers, on the grounds that protection could be provided by a 'majority clan'.

Quasi-state entities controlling part of a territory are often, by their very nature, temporary and unstable, as has been seen in Somalia. The very authority of these bodies over the territory may be disputed. In addition, such bodies are not parties to international human-rights instruments and are therefore unaccountable in international law. In spite of this, some member states have rejected claims by Somali asylum seekers, on the grounds that protection could be provided by a 'majority clan'.

International organisations are also likely to have limited control and authority over the territory in question, as was seen in Srebrenica in 1995, where a massacre occurred after the town had been designated in 1993 as a United Nations Safe Area. They will not be able to carry out the full functions of a state over the full territory of a state. In addition, the accountability of such organisations in international human-rights law is far from clear.[12] It is therefore inappropriate to present such bodies as realistic sources of effective, durable protection. Despite this, member states have argued that UNMIK forces in Kosovo could be considered to be protection providers. As seen in the Democratic Republic of Congo (DRC), however, UN bodies are often unable to provide effective, durable protection to civilians (see Box 1).

Box 1 Bunia after Artemis: non-state agents of protection?

'Even with MONUC here, people are afraid of the lawlessness in the city centre. We have the impression that MONUC would not put themselves on the line. The soldiers will freely tell you that they didn't come to the Congo to die.'

A review of efforts to provide security to civilians in the Democratic Republic of Congo – especially through the EU's Operation Artemis and the United Nations Mission in the DRC (MONUC) – provides important insights into the challenges facing 'non-state agents of protection'.

The DRC, with a population of 58 million, is held together tenuously by a transitional government which was consolidated in 2003. The eastern part of the country, rich in resources and bordering conflict-ridden Rwanda, Burundi, and Uganda, has traditionally been the crux of fighting which reportedly claimed the lives of some 3.3 million people between 1998 and 2002.[13]

It was in Ituri in eastern DRC, in early 2003, that reports of massacres, rapes, and cannibalism received worldwide attention. Since 1999, Ituri has been racked by a devastating conflict which has claimed the lives of more than 55,000 civilians and caused more than 500,000 people to flee from their homes.[14] Uruguayan MONUC troops watched helplessly in May 2003 as thousands of residents fled during bloody fighting in the town of Bunia. In response, the United Nations passed Security Council Resolution 1484, authorising a Chapter VII intervention in Bunia to protect UN staff and assets, as well as civilians, until MONUC could reinforce its presence.[15] The European Union responded with the three-month Operation Artemis, a Multi-national Intervention Force (MNF) under French command. Artemis, with 2200 soldiers from 17 countries, was the first military mission fielded by the EU outside Europe.[16]

According to the civilians interviewed for this report, Operation Artemis successfully averted the immediate threat of violence in Bunia. However, atrocities continued outside Bunia town, and the operation's limited period and mandate of deployment meant that many militia leaders remained active. As one observer noted, its successor, the MONUC contingent, inherited a much more challenging task: '*Artemis put the lid on a boiling pot. MONUC has to stop the pot from boiling.*'[17]

When Artemis departed in September 2003, additional MONUC forces arrived, with a new Chapter VII mandate which allowed them to use weapons to protect the population. There are 4700 military personnel in Ituri, deployed in seven locations outside Bunia.[18] Lack of clarity regarding interpretation and implementation of MONUC's Chapter VII mandate is one of the mission's biggest frustrations to date. According to interviewees in Kinshasa, Goma, and Bunia, the decision-making mechanisms and modalities of using force are ill-defined. Commanders can, and do, overrule actions that might endanger their troops.

MONUC's resources are considered seriously inadequate for the job at hand. The scope of its mandate, and its unspecific nature, make it difficult to allocate the available resources effectively. The new ceiling of 16,700 personnel, provided by Security Council Resolution 1565, falls well short of the 23,900 troops and 507 civilian staff that Secretary General Kofi Annan had recommended.[19] Lack of funds and equipment prevents regular patrols on lakes along the border. At the most basic level, most troops cannot speak French, which severely limits their ability to communicate on the ground or to collect intelligence.

Agents of protection or perpetrators of abuse?

To make matters worse, MONUC troops have been accused of exploiting and abusing women and girls whom they are mandated to protect. In May 2004, a report in *The Independent* stated: 'Mothers as young as 13, the victims of multiple rapes by militiamen, can only secure enough food to survive in the Bunia IDP camp by sleeping with Moroccan and Uruguayan soldiers.'[20] A UN oversight mission assigned to investigate the alleged abuse uncovered 'serious allegations of sexual exploitation and misconduct by MONUC civilian and military personnel in Bunia, consisting mainly of prostitution but also including incidents of rape'.[21] In a report to the General Assembly, Secretary General Annan reiterated the UN's 'zero tolerance' policy and outlined a 'rapid response action plan' to address the issue internally. However, justice for the survivors is still administered on an *ad hoc* basis, at best. Under UN regulations, final authority to prosecute the accused perpetrators rests with the troop-sending country. The UN itself cannot monitor the treatment of these cases, or ensure that implicated individuals are not transferred to service elsewhere in the world.

Bunia one year later

In the light of the intensive efforts to improve conditions in this small corner of the Congo, it is worth considering how civilians perceive their security one year after Artemis forces first arrived. Generally, daytime security has improved in Bunia, and the markets and other businesses function – a big improvement on the situation in mid-2003. However, as of mid-2004, Bunia continued to be divided between the predominantly Northern Hema (or Gegere) groups and the Lendu neighbourhoods to the south. Most people feel uncomfortable moving from one section to another, if they feel they are from an ethnic group which may be targeted in the wrong part of town, so they stay indoors after 8 pm. As one resident explained, *'Even with MONUC here, people are afraid of the lawlessness in the city centre. We have the impression that MONUC would not put themselves on the line. The soldiers will freely tell you that they didn't come to the Congo to die.'*

As of August 2004, around 66,000 persons displaced from Bunia were living in the Beni area, most of them waiting for improved security to allow them to return. A very clear indicator is the continued existence of the IDP camp in Bunia: most of the inhabitants are from Bunia, but they do not feel it is safe to leave the security of the camp for their homes, which are sometimes only a few hundred metres away. Bunia itself hosted around 56,000 individuals displaced from surrounding villages. This number excludes the 12,600 residents of Camp Aero, the biggest IDP settlement in the city.[22] Conditions in the camp are cramped and difficult; but, as a 46-year-old IDP in the camp told us, *'Those displaced out of the camp are a bit forgotten. At least here you get something to eat from time to time. And it's harder for someone to get you out of bed and kill you.'*

If civilians in Bunia have barely attained a modicum of security and justice, the vast majority of Congolese in the east are in an even more precarious position. Large swathes of North and South Kivu and Maniema provinces are inaccessible to humanitarian agencies, on account of continuing hostilities or the threat of attack. Forest dwellers and other displaced people are especially isolated. Although international agencies have succeeded in negotiating access on a piecemeal basis, major obstacles to the delivery of aid and protection remain.

The Procedures Directive

The Procedures Directive [23] prescribes the procedures for deciding asylum claims that are made in the EU. Within this, it sets out criteria for labelling certain countries as 'safe', potentially in contravention of international refugee-protection principles.

Wide divergences between the asylum systems in different member states made agreement of this Directive extremely difficult, and protracted negotiations drove standards down[24] to such an extreme low level that the UN High Commissioner for Refugees (UNHCR) and others took the exceptional measure of calling for the draft Directive to be taken off the table. As the High Commissioner himself stated: 'If Member States' main preoccupation is to ensure that the Directive includes exceptions which safeguard their own national asylum provisions and objectives, I fear that this Directive will be reduced to a catalogue of optional provisions, including significant departures from accepted international refugee and human rights law.'[25]

A number of key clauses threaten to contravene refugee and human-rights law, in particular those concerning 'safe countries'. The idea of 'safe countries' is not new. Many states keep 'white lists' of countries which they consider safe, so that the claims of asylum seekers coming through or from these countries can be labelled 'manifestly unfounded'. Member states may then, after only a limited hearing, remove or return these people. The Procedures Directive goes further, because it removes the right to *any* hearing for some asylum seekers who have travelled through 'safe third countries'. It also obliges all member states to adopt a common list of 'safe countries of origin'.

An asylum seeker who has entered or sought to enter the EU illegally, after transit through a 'safe third country', could be denied access to an asylum procedure in the EU altogether. This raises serious threats to asylum seekers' rights to a fair hearing and to the fundamental international principle of non-refoulement. This legal obligation, which requires states not to send any person back to a situation where he or she may suffer persecution, is a fundamental rule of international law.[26]

Asylum seekers will have no opportunity to rebut the presumption that the 'third' country they have passed through is 'safe' in their particular case; nor will member states be obliged to obtain assurances that the third country concerned will process the asylum claim.[27] This could have severe consequences for the individuals concerned, because asylum seekers transferred from the EU to a third country may then be sent back to their country of origin without any assessment of their protection needs. Using the broad criteria in the Directive, such safe countries could potentially include the Russian Federation and the Ukraine. International organisations have often expressed fundamental protection-related concerns in these countries.[28]

The 'safe third-country' provisions threaten two important principles. They mean that asylum seekers could be returned to places where they may not be safe. They also threaten to shift the responsibility for hosting and processing asylum claims to poorer countries outside the EU which have less well-resourced asylum infrastructure, or none at all. These provisions could therefore be used in conjunction with recent proposals to process asylum claims overseas. They could create a means of removing large numbers of asylum seekers to processing camps in countries such as Libya and the Ukraine (see Chapter 6).

Asylum seekers transferred from the EU to a third country may be sent back to their country of origin without any assessment of their protection needs.

Not all EU countries currently have a list of safe countries of origin (SCOs), but the Procedures Directive provides for a binding common list, and obliges all member states to consider claims by people from listed countries as 'unfounded'.[29] These applications can then be put through an accelerated procedure. The burden of proof will rest entirely on asylum seekers, who will be required to rebut this presumption of safety. The Council may amend the common list, after consultation (i.e. not 'co-decision') with the European Parliament. However, the Directive imposes no obligation to conduct regular, updated analyses of the continuing 'safety' of these countries.[30]

In 2004, member states and the Commission tried to draw up this common list, but their proposed designations were so strongly contested that they agreed to postpone the finalisation of the list until after the Procedures Directive was adopted. The countries proposed for inclusion in 2004 were Benin, Botswana, Cape Verde, Chile, Costa Rica, Ghana, Mali, Mauritius, Senegal, and Uruguay. Each member state was asked to assess each potential SCO individually, and give its opinion.

Neither UNHCR, nor any NGO, was present at the meeting of the Asylum Working Group when the SCO list was being negotiated in mid-2004. The information proposed by the Commission and the Presidency for these negotiations was inadequate. Very few independent bodies were represented on the suggested list of sources, and many of the suggested reports were four or even five years out of date. Some reports were written in 1996.[31] Some member states relied on additional information received from sources which could not be revealed for reasons of diplomacy. This lack of transparency is a cause for concern, given the significant consequences for many asylum seekers if a third country is placed on the SCO list.

Diplomatic considerations and concerns about numbers of asylum seekers dominated the discussions, and there were widely differing opinions regarding the safety of certain countries. Reports indicate that the Commission opposed including any of the seven African countries on the list, while some member states were opposed to including four of these, and others supported the inclusion of all of them.[32]

Apart from the lack of transparency and the poor quality of information used, the very idea that a country can be deemed safe for everyone is problematic. It runs counter to the principle of asylum and the reality that individuals and certain groups may face persecution in seemingly safe places, and that 'safe' places may become rapidly 'unsafe'.

Box 2 'No war, no peace' in Sri Lanka

'Lots of families are hiding their kids at home, in forests, or they keep changing locations. If they're a bit well off, they'll go to a relative in another village. If they're even better off, they'll go further away. Single mothers especially have no contacts. They are the ones whose daughters live in the forest. There's definitely a lot of fear, and it's justified.'

The situation in Sri Lanka shows the difficulties inherent in making a reliable judgement on the safety of a country. Although conditions there have dramatically improved, the situation has been described as a state of 'no war, no peace'. It is impossible to deem it safe for everyone, for three reasons: because the peace is fragile and conditions are so changeable; because some groups are still at risk; and because it is impossible to know the situation in all parts of the country.

A fragile peace

More than 20 years of civil war in Sri Lanka have cost at least 64,000 lives and displaced nearly one million people.[33] Since the government of Sri Lanka and the Liberation Tigers of Tamil Eelam (LTTE) agreed to a ceasefire in 2002, serious human-rights abuses perpetrated by government security forces have markedly declined.[34] However, violence and intimidation continue to permeate people's lives, especially in the northern and eastern parts of the country.[35] A protection officer for an international NGO remarked, *'You can't call this post-conflict. It's conflict with another name and played in another way.'*

Human-rights reports since the ceasefire have documented acts of forced recruitment, abductions, torture in custody, extortion by non-state actors, repression of free speech, and political killings. By the end of 2003, UNHCR offices recorded more than 40 post-ceasefire cases of suspected political killings.[36] Indeed, the civilians to whom Oxfam spoke in Kilinochchi, Vavuniya, Trincomalee, and Batticaloa unanimously expressed a sense of impending collapse of the ceasefire, which in fact has made no progress since late 2003. One human-rights activist observed, *'The problem is that we have seen so many ceasefire agreements fail, including under this President.*

We have yet to find a permanent solution.' In the village of Wadduvan West, a 36-year-old Tamil fisherman commented, *'We are expecting the war to start again. When it does, we will take our fibre boats, our nets, a lamp, matches, and a few clothes across the river. Since the Memorandum of Understanding, we've fixed our house and bought chickens and cows. Now we've stopped buying things, because we're afraid the peace process will collapse.'*

Political events since early 2004 have seriously threatened prospects for lasting peace: there has been a parliamentary power struggle in Colombo, and the LTTE commander in the East, Colonel Karuna, has split off from the main Tamil Tiger organisation. On 9 April, the main LTTE faction launched an attack and quickly defeated Karuna's forces. However, certain areas are still under Karuna's influence, and a low-intensity conflict between the factions continues, resulting in deaths and displacement of civilians. According to military sources, about 20 people were killed in the original battle between the two sides. Meanwhile, approximately 11,000 civilians had pre-emptively displaced themselves and taken refuge, mainly with friends and relatives in nearby communities.[37]

This 'no war, no peace' situation has been affected by the massive devastation wrought along approximately 80 per cent of the Sri Lankan coastline by the tsunami of 26 December 2004. At the time of writing (January 2005), more than 800,000 people have been left homeless and more than 31,000 are known to have died. Temporary displacement camps have been set up, and security and protection issues are quickly becoming manifest. While this tragedy has affected all communities, the east – where communities were already extremely vulnerable, due to dislocation and the effects of the conflict, and also to the impact of severe flooding which occurred less than one month before the tsunami struck – was exceptionally hard hit (especially Ampara, Batticalaoa, and Mullaitivu districts). The full impact of the disaster on the dynamics of the conflict is not yet known, but initial general optimism that this shared tragedy could bring communities together is already being challenged, as tensions generated by the chronic conflict are played out in the politics that govern the control of aid and resources flowing into different parts of the country. In the direct aftermath of the tsunami, UNHCR called for governments to suspend involuntary returns of failed asylum seekers to all affected countries, including Sri Lanka: a call which at the time of writing had been heeded by some EU governments.

Still at risk: children, deserters, and dissidents

Fallout from the Karuna split continues to threaten stability in the East. Karuna supporters and other political opponents of the LTTE have been murdered in significant numbers – more than one dozen in June 2004 alone.[38] Furthermore, former Karuna cadres, including children, are being aggressively recruited by the LTTE in an effort to replenish its ranks. A resident of Batticaloa described conditions there: *'Lots of families are hiding their kids at home, in forests, or they keep changing locations. If they're a bit well off, they'll go to a relative in another village. If they're even better off, they'll go further away. Single mothers especially have no contacts. They are the ones whose daughters live in the forest. There's definitely a lot of fear, and it's justified.'*

From March to May 2004, for example, the number of recruits reported to UNICEF jumped from 29 to 96.[39] Service providers emphasise that such figures represent a fraction of the reality, as most families with an interest in releasing their children go directly to the LTTE. According to UNICEF in Kilinochchi, no Tamil child in the north or east is immune to the threat of recruitment. Most cadres do, however, come from vulnerable families: welfare centres hosting 'up-country Tamils' are considered fertile recruitment grounds for the LTTE. These are Tamils of hill-country origin who have been resident, often without land ownership, in Kilinochchi and Mullaitivu districts, and they are some of the most marginalised of the IDPs. For teenagers and young adults from disadvantaged backgrounds, the movement offers economic benefits, a sense of security, and a chance to fight – literally – against social and economic injustice. As one service provider explained, *'Let's say I am hungry. You tell me there is too much food on your table and invite me to join. Will I just sit, or will I take some? It's better to die for a cause than from hunger.'*

Girls, who comprise 43 per cent of the recruits, face particular challenges.[40] Sometimes their families will reject them out of shame, especially if their decision to join was voluntary. Numerous female ex-cadres interviewed for this study said they felt bad to appear in public, because their tanned skin and cropped haircuts revealed their history. Some parents marry their daughters off early as a form of protection.

Young adults who fall outside UNICEF's mandate are also vulnerable. An observer from the Scandinavian-led Sri Lanka Monitoring Mission (SLMM), which oversees the ceasefire, explained: '*Youths are promised work and education and suddenly they find themselves in the middle of the jungle. Those that escape cannot stay at home. They would be re-recruited ...and no one can protect the deserters over the age of eighteen.*' [41]

Finally, the LTTE targets people, regardless of age, who express opposition to the movement. According to the UN Human Rights Advisor in Sri Lanka, '*For anyone with a dissident Tamil profile, there is no place of security. The LTTE can strike at any time, anywhere in the country.*' Members of Tamil groups such as the EPDP, PLOTE, and ENDLF are especially at risk. Moreover, the passage of time does not seem to reduce the danger. Dissenters are terrified of persecution, even if the triggering event that created their risk took place years, even decades, ago. A peace activist in Batticaloa told us: '*At least the security forces were a recognised group. The LTTE are part of the community and are completely unaccountable.*'

The challenge of communication

'*So many people suffered, so many families have disappeared. People are not secure about their own life and cannot criticise anything.*'
Service provider, Trincomalee

The situation in Sri Lanka is complex and fluid – qualities which are difficult to capture and communicate to audiences in Colombo, much less to policy makers in Brussels or other European capitals. According to a UN staff person based in Trincomalee: '*People in Colombo think the war has ended. I have to remind them,"Well, yes, but grenade attacks, suicide bombings, hartals [work strikes which often lead to violence and heightened security measures], and assassinations continue up here".*' Many people working in the north and east expressed frustration with the lack of communication between the capital and their districts. While events are documented in numerous situation reports, and discussed at co-ordination meetings in Colombo, there exists a sense that the fragility of the peace is not adequately acknowledged. '*Everyone wants a success story*', explained one observer.

One reason why it is difficult to communicate the actual levels of violence and coercion is because affected people are reluctant to report their experiences. Most civilians, particularly in remote LTTE-controlled communities, are too fearful to condemn the Tigers openly. The LTTE's selective recruitment tactics reinforce this fear. For example, when only a handful of children are taken from a village, unaffected families keep quiet, rather than draw attention to their own good fortune. Although a few groups of cadre mothers have directly challenged the LTTE, there is no large-scale organised resistance movement.

Local leaders do not dare to challenge the LTTE too explicitly in public. A prominent community organiser in Vavuniya observed, '*We know who the killers are, but still we say "unidentified gunman" in our reports*'. In government-controlled areas in the north and east, lawyers are afraid to file cases against the LTTE, and '*magistrates who have discretion don't use it*'.[42] It may also be the case that police are unable or unwilling to investigate killings, making it difficult to attribute deaths reliably to ceasefire violations.

Cultural attitudes also discourage direct dialogue. Civilians are especially reticent to share their troubles with outsiders. As one service provider noted, '*Everyone has a story, everyone's been affected, but Tamils are very careful about what they reveal to foreigners. People have had their entire families gunned down and they won't tell you.*' One Sri Lankan human-rights activist expressed her frustration with this tendency to remain silent: '*Why can't we talk about what's wrong with our society that thousands of children are taken?*'

Even service providers in the north and east feel obliged to keep quiet. Because the LTTE leadership has enforced numerous restrictions on (particularly local) NGOs, relatively few agencies implement extensive programmes in areas under its control. Of those that do, most believe that their mere presence has a deterrent effect on abusers. Still, not all feel free to challenge authorities on the basis of what their beneficiaries report: '*In trying to meet basic needs, space for political discussion has shrunk. If people want to build wells and latrines, they agree not to speak out.*' [43]

The need for accurate information

Sound information on countries of origin (COI) is an essential element of national asylum systems, and the quality of COI is an indicator of states' willingness and capacity to understand refugee realities elsewhere. If states do not base their own procedures on solid information, there is little hope for the far more ambitious and complex plans such as extra-territorial processing and 'orderly entry' procedures.

The provisions in the Qualifications and Procedures directives go to the heart of the need for EU claims about conditions in third countries to be based on comprehensive, reliable, and current sources of information. As we have seen, the country information provided during negotiations about the 'safe countries' lists has been far from adequate.

Refugee-status determination (RSD) cannot be properly carried out without accurate and up-to-date COI. According to UNHCR guidelines, RSD entails an assessment of both objective and subjective elements – i.e. what does the individual fear? And does the available COI suggest that this fear is reasonable, given the country conditions and the individual's own circumstances? [44] For asylum seekers not entitled to refugee status under the 1951 Convention, accurate COI is crucial, because such persons may still face other dangers if returned home, and they therefore have a pressing case for humanitarian protection.

For purposes of consistency, and to ensure that 'protection gaps' do not exist between the asylum systems in different EU member states, all EU members must be able to access, and indeed share with each other, reliable information on asylum seekers' countries of origin and transit. The difficulties encountered in drawing up a list of 'safe countries of origin' indicate that this is not the case at present. There are also wide divergences in acceptance rates for certain groups in different European countries. In the first three months of 2004, 96 per cent of Russian nationals (the vast majority of whom were Chechen) were granted asylum in Austria; in both 2003 and 2004, none of this group was accepted in Slovakia.[45]

All EU members must be able to access, and share with each other, reliable information on asylum seekers' countries of origin and transit.

There have been some efforts to share COI between member states, notably through EURASIL (the European Union Network for Asylum Practitioners). EURASIL was created in mid-2002, is supervised by the European Commission, and meets six to eight times per year. The meetings are attended by the asylum authorities of each member state, and by representatives from the Commission. The stated purpose is to strengthen the working relationship between EU asylum practitioners, and to facilitate the sharing of information and experience. Information is shared about conditions in countries of origin and transit, and about practical issues of conducting RSD in the EU. Individual meetings may have a specific geographical focus (i.e. to share information on a particular country of origin), and/or a thematic focus.

According to the Commission, international organisations such as UNHCR, IOM, and ICRC are invited to EURASIL meetings 'from time to time', and 'for particular topics'. EURASIL meetings could, therefore, provide an opportunity to share information between international organisations/ NGOs and EU policy makers. The record of EURASIL, however, is generally negative. NGOs have criticised the lack of transparency with which EURASIL operates. Insufficient time is given to seek out the requested information for a forthcoming EURASIL meeting, and IGOs / NGOs are given no insight into whether the information that they present at the meeting is accepted by those present. If their information is rejected, no explanation is given, and the source of any contrary information is not disclosed.

The poor quality of EU co-operation reflects the poor quality of member-states' COI, and the reality that many asylum seekers in the EU are having their applications judged on the basis of flawed information. EU governments have been criticised for their use of inaccurate and outdated information. It has been found that EU member states often quote selectively from NGO reports in such a way as to paint an unduly optimistic picture of certain countries.[46] In the light of the serious flaws in the current system of providing COI, the UK House of Lords has called for an independent documentation centre, not only for the UK but also on an EU-wide basis.[47]

Recommendations

Principles

- Asylum seekers have the right to have their claims individually examined by means of a full and fair procedure. This should be the cornerstone of EU asylum policy, regardless of asylum seekers' country of origin and/or transit and their method of entry to the EU.
- No country can be considered safe for all of its citizens. EU lists of 'safe countries' should not be drawn up.
- Non-state agents cannot guarantee to fulfil the duties of a state, and should not be considered as realistic sources of effective, durable protection from persecution for the purposes of asylum.

Application

- When transposing the Directives of the first stage of the Common European Asylum System (CEAS), EU member states must strive to exceed minimum standards and meet their commitment, made at Tampere, to fully respect and fulfil their international obligations. On no account should they lower their existing standards towards the minimum.
- In developing the second stage of the CEAS, EU member states must meet the commitment made in The Hague Programme to a 'full and inclusive application of the Geneva Convention on Refugees and other relevant treaties'.
- EU policy makers in each institution should establish a more structured and transparent approach to consultation on asylum, involving independent experts – including NGOs and UNHCR. In particular the Council of the EU should create a framework for consultation, the Commission should formalise current forums, and the European Parliament should continue to undertake meaningful dialogue with stakeholder groups.
- In the short term, the Commission should increase the transparency of EURASIL meetings, to allow information to be shared between member states and independent experts.

- In the medium to long term, EU leaders should explore the possibility of establishing an independent Country of Origin Information (COI) documentation centre, with adequate resources to ensure accurate and up-to-date information. This should be complemented by a mechanism for independent scrutiny of COI.
- High-quality COI must be accompanied by high-quality training of immigration officials, to ensure that the information is used to make sound decisions in asylum cases.
- In countries of origin, international, national, and local agencies should continue efforts to streamline the monitoring and communication of human-rights violations. EU and member-state delegations should create forums in which these agencies, as well as affected individuals, can channel current and accurate information to European COI mechanisms.

On the edges of the EU: 'managing migration' from Europe's neighbours

4

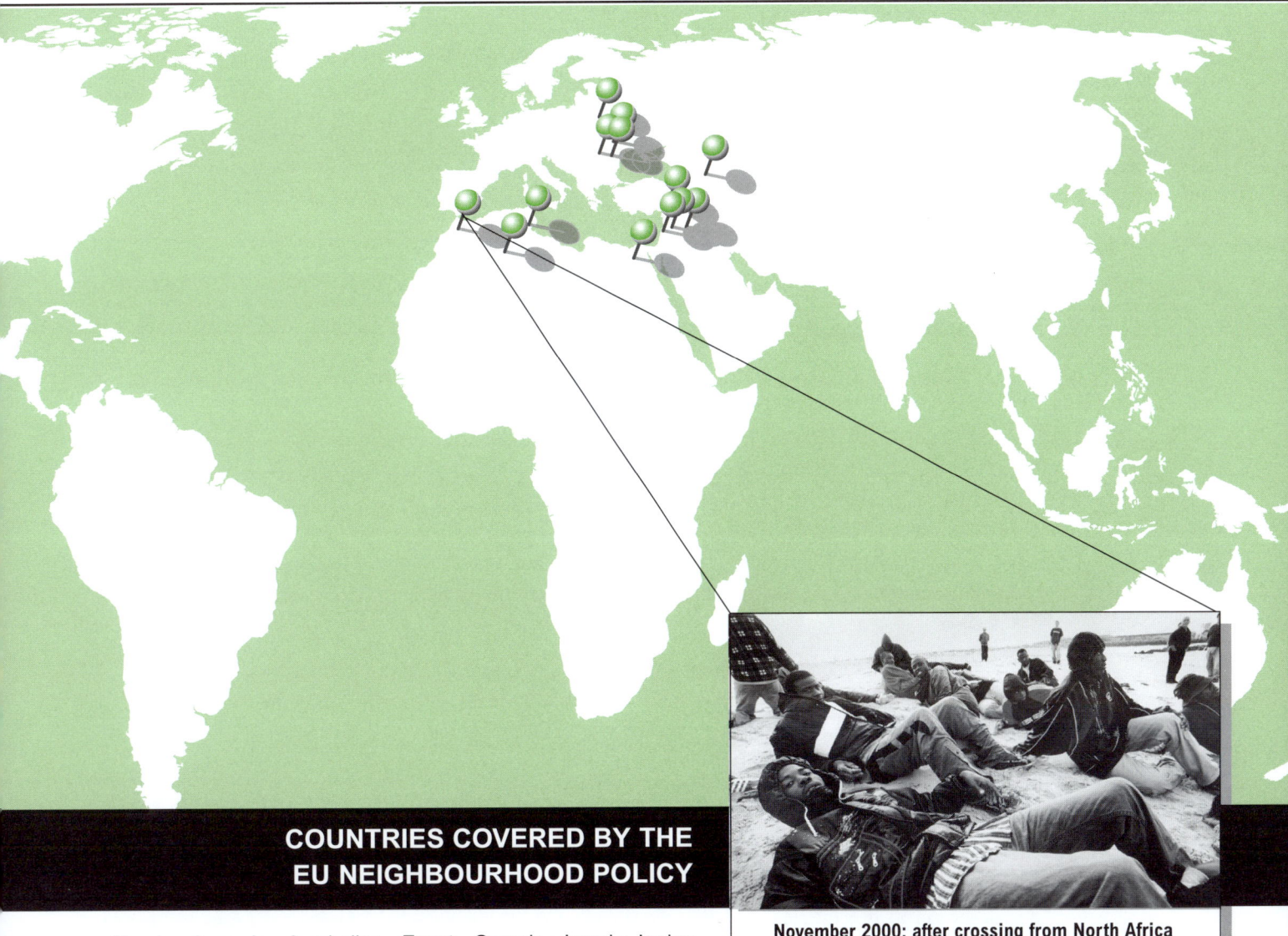

COUNTRIES COVERED BY THE EU NEIGHBOURHOOD POLICY

Algeria • Armenia • Azerbaijan • Egypt • Georgia • Israel • Jordan
Lebanon • Moldova • Morocco • Palestinian Authority • Tunisia • Ukraine

November 2000: after crossing from North Africa by boat, would-be immigrants sit in the sand on the beach of Tarifa, Spain
© Juan Carlos Tomasi

4
On the edges of the EU: 'managing migration' from Europe's neighbours

> *'When refugees cannot seek asylum because of offshore barriers, or are detained for excessive periods in unsatisfactory conditions, or are refused entry because of restrictive interpretations of the Convention, the asylum system is broken, and the promise of the Convention is broken, too.'*
>
> Kofi Annan, UN Secretary General, Address to the European Parliament, 29 January 2004

Controlling access – borders, barriers, and interception

Managing migration or providing protection?

EU states are increasing their investment in an array of measures designed to control entry into EU territory. These measures are seen as necessary to 'manage migration' and prevent irregular entry. However, they have the effect of blocking safe and legal ways for asylum seekers to access protection in EU member states, forcing them into dangerous situations. The migration-management agenda and set of policy tools are central to the 'internationalisation' of EU asylum policy. The list of policy tools is long and growing. This chapter will examine a few of the measures employed: border controls, immigration liaison officers, interception at sea, and sanctions on carriers.

From the late 1990s, as European governments recognised that a complete end to immigration was neither desirable nor feasible, they began to speak of 'migration management'. This phrase, frequently heard in European governments and institutions, seems to be a guiding principle in the development of EU asylum policies. A broad consensus developed across some states and institutions which viewed migration as inevitable and necessary for demographic and economic reasons, and its management essential. Nonetheless, with a few exceptions, governments in Europe have been slow to create legal channels for labour migration, and some continued to restrict opportunities for family reunion. However, in the absence of adequate formal channels, pulled by the demand for labour in Europe and pushed by the poverty outside it, many people enter the EU via irregular migration channels. Their presence in Europe exacerbates an already highly politicised issue which touches on fears about race, national identity, security, employment, and welfare. Ill-considered political pronouncements, hostile expressions of public opinion, and biased media reporting have contributed to the rise of political extremism in some countries, and unease and discrimination in many.

Asylum seekers are caught up in this movement of irregular migrants, because they have virtually no 'regular' way of reaching EU territory. Many of the measures put in place by governments target asylum seekers, since it is presumed that the majority have no legitimate claim to protection. This chapter explores the impact of some of these measures on the ability of people to seek protection.

Criminalising the right to seek asylum

For a person seeking to exercise his or her right to asylum, the first step is being able to access and live in safe territory while his or her case is being decided. Asylum seekers must not be turned away from EU territory before their case has been decided, or prevented from reaching it in the first place. A common EU asylum system will become meaningless if EU member states prevent asylum seekers from accessing it. UNHCR has made it clear that the principle of non-refoulement applies at the moment at which asylum seekers present themselves for entry. That is, it encompasses both non-return *and* non-rejection at the frontier.[1] Consequently, the UNHCR Agenda for Protection asserts as follows:

> *States are encouraged to ensure that any immigration control measures they adopt contain safeguards allowing access to international protection for those who need it. These kinds of safeguards should also be applied during rescue-at-sea operations and during any attempts to intercept migrants before they reach their intended destinations.* [2]

To ensure that people fleeing violence and persecution did not get caught up in the nets of 'migration management', European leaders committed themselves at Tampere to *'the absolute respect of the right to seek asylum'* and stated that common policies on asylum and migration would offer guarantees to those who seek protection in or access to the European Union, while taking into account the need to combat illegal immigration. The European Commission has also urged that 'measures relating to the fight against illegal immigration have to balance the right to decide whether to accord or refuse admission to the territory to third country nationals and the obligation to protect those genuinely in need of international protection'.[3] This balance has not been achieved, and protection has taken second place to the fight against illegal immigration.

European leaders committed themselves at Tampere to 'the absolute respect of the right to seek asylum'.

With deterrence rather than protection being the priority for most member states, seeking asylum in the EU has become increasingly difficult, in spite of the EU's frequently articulated commitment to the 1951 Refugee Convention. These actions have effectively blocked access to Europe, to the extent that it is now virtually impossible for asylum seekers to enter Europe legally.[4] It is estimated that 90 per cent of asylum seekers have to rely on illegal entry methods to enter EU territory.[5] More and more asylum seekers are forced to rely on smugglers and traffickers – an outcome which the EU had specifically pledged to avoid. More than 5000 deaths of refugees and migrants caused by these 'Fortress Europe' policies have been documented,[6] and many more remain undocumented. This is the dilemma[7] facing many people who wish to seek protection in Europe.

Controlling the borders of the enlarged EU: few safeguards for refugees

The Tampere European Council called for closer co-operation and mutual technical assistance between member states' border-control services, 'especially on maritime borders', and for the rapid inclusion of the (then) applicant states in this collaboration. As new member states have joined the EU, its external borders have shifted eastwards.

The EU has collectively spent huge sums on a range of border-control and interception measures, including increased numbers of border guards; helicopters with heat detectors; high-speed patrol boats; infra-red detection devices and night-vision equipment; movement detectors to search for stowaways in lorries; x-ray scanners; satellites to monitor cross-border movement (currently under discussion); and biometrics and fingerprinting equipment.

In addition, EU-wide initiatives have been taken specifically to co-ordinate border-control measures. In October 2004, the Council established a European Border Management Agency[8] to integrate the management of the external borders of the EU, with the long-term goal of establishing an EU Border Police. The relevant Regulation makes no reference to the right to seek asylum.[9] This could have serious consequences: if such a body is to oversee EU border management, it must distinguish between persons in need of international protection and other migrants. Otherwise, asylum seekers arriving at EU borders may be summarily sent back to a situation where their life or safety would be in jeopardy.

Interception measures rarely differentiate between people who may be in need of international protection and other migrants.

Interception measures: divesting responsibility for protection

Interception measures are essentially border-control measures which are applied before a person reaches the physical border of an EU member state. The aim is to block the access to member-state territory of any undocumented person crossing international borders by land, air, or sea. Interception measures can be applied within the country of departure, in the transit country, within territorial waters, or on the high seas. To date, many of these measures have been undertaken unilaterally by individual member states, although recently there have been moves towards collective EU action.

Interception measures are presented as an important tool in the fight against illegal migration, but they rarely differentiate between people who may be in need of international protection and other migrants. In some cases, potential asylum seekers intercepted on their way to the EU have been sent directly back to countries where their life or freedom will be in danger.

Member states often refuse to accept responsibility for meeting the protection needs of people affected by these actions. This attitude, however, is contrary to general principles of international law, according to which:

- state responsibility may arise directly from the acts of government officials and agents, or indirectly where the domestic systems fail to enforce or guarantee the observance of international standards;[10]

- and a state's obligations under international law extend beyond its physical territory. The fact that the action of a state takes place outside the territory of that state, or causes harm outside of that territory, in no way diminishes the responsibility of that state for that action.[11]

The principle of non-refoulement must also govern extra-territorial actions by a State. As UNHCR's Standing Committee concluded:

> *The principle of non-refoulement does not imply any geographical limitation. [...] obligations extend to all government agents acting in an official capacity, within or outside national territory. [...] Interception and other enforcement measures should take into account the fundamental difference, under international law, between refugees and asylum-seekers who are entitled to international protection, and other migrants who can resort to the protection of their country of origin.*[12]

Immigration Liaison Officers: ignoring asylum claims

Since the late 1990s, EU member states have posted immigration liaison officers (ILOs) in countries from which they hope to curb emigration or onward movement to Europe. The Regulation dated February 2004, which established an EU ILO Network, defines ILOs as representatives of member states, posted in third countries 'with a view to contributing to the prevention and combating of illegal immigration, the return of illegal immigrants and the management of legal migration'. However, this Regulation contains no specific provisions related to protection of refugees or asylum seekers' rights under international refugee law.[13]

Some member states did not wait for the EU to finalise common rules and procedures; they have acted unilaterally or bilaterally. While these interception policies aim primarily to combat irregular immigration, they also pose formidable barriers for asylum seekers. If EU member states implement such measures without adequate safeguards for persons in need of international protection, they risk breaching their obligations under international law.

Box 3 UK immigration officers in Prague Airport: targeting asylum seekers

In July 2001, the UK introduced a 'pre-clearance' procedure in Prague. By agreement with the Czech government, UK immigration officers were posted in Prague airport. The stated aim was to actively prevent any would-be Czech (Roma) asylum-seekers boarding a plane to the UK and seeking asylum there. The UK justified this initiative by referring to the relatively low level of acceptance rates for those Czech nationals (specifically Roma) who sought asylum in the UK.[14]

The Czech nationals who were intercepted were not given any kind of substantive asylum hearing by the UK immigration officers in Prague. UK authorities argued that, as they had not yet left their country of origin at the time of their interception, they could not be classified as refugees and therefore did not benefit from the rights conferred by the 1951 Convention.

Unsurprisingly, the legality of this practice was challenged by NGOs. In a recent judgement, the British House of Lords found that the UK was indeed acting in a discriminatory manner against Roma in Prague Airport.

However, the Lords did not find the pre-clearance procedures to be contrary to the UK's obligations under the 1951 Convention; they rejected the arguments of UNHCR, and concluded that the principle of *non-refoulement* does not have extra-territorial effect.[15]

This judgement, effectively, has declared it legal for a signatory state of the 1951 Refugee Convention to *actively* obstruct the attempts of would-be asylum seekers to leave their country of origin and gain access to that state's asylum procedures. In Oxfam's view, the UK's procedures in Prague airport were, in fact, contrary to the object and purpose (if not the very letter) of international refugee law. Such procedures, if replicated on a wide scale, would make the 1951 Convention meaningless. As UNHCR has commented: 'Given the practice of States to intercept persons at great distance from their own territory, the international refugee protection regime would be rendered ineffective if States' agents abroad were free to act at variance with obligations under international refugee law and human rights law'.[16]

Interception at sea

EU member states have also discussed the possibility of joint patrols and the possible interception of migrants in the central and eastern Mediterranean. Several members, including Malta and Cyprus, have already given political support to the 'Neptune Plan', which would include not only sea patrolling, but also repatriation measures through co-operation with countries of origin and transit.

Member states have also engaged in numerous interception projects multilaterally, though not necessarily in an EU framework. These include 'Operation Ulysses' (to reduce illegal immigration by sea in the northern Mediterranean, involving the UK, France, Italy, and Portugal); 'Operation Triton' (operation in the south-eastern Mediterranean, involving Greece, Spain, France, Italy, UK, Cyprus, and Malta); and 'Project Deniz' (a project to intercept migrants in Turkish seas, led by the UK). In addition, EU member states are establishing two sea-border centres, in Greece and in Spain, to oversee the implementation of a sea-border programme.[17]

Given the precedents for such operations, these plans are a cause for concern. The interception of asylum seekers at sea often leads to an assessment of protection needs which is cursory and inadequate at best, and sometimes non-existent. Sometimes the result has been refoulement. This was seen in the case of the refoulement of Eritreans by Malta in late 2003 (see Box 4).

The interception of asylum seekers at sea often leads to an assessment of protection needs which is cursory and inadequate at best, and sometimes non-existent.

More recently, in July 2004, 37 African asylum seekers were forced to make a three-week voyage across the Mediterranean aboard a German aid ship, the *Cap Anamur*. Italy refused to let the ship dock, arguing that it was closer to Malta, and that the people on board should apply for asylum there. After a 21-day *impasse,* the ship was finally allowed to dock in Sicily, where the asylum seekers were placed in a holding centre for illegal immigrants, without access to legal counsel. Even before they had been interviewed, Italian authorities declared that no one in the group was a refugee. Even after the Italian Central Commission for Refugees recommended that 22 people from the group be allowed to stay for humanitarian reasons, 'most, if not all, of the group were nevertheless deported' on 22 July. UNHCR was given limited access to the group in Sicily, and has criticised the process in Sicily for falling short not only of international norms, but also of accepted European standards.[18]

Further controversy arose in October 2004, when hundreds of asylum seekers landed on the Italian island of Lampedusa. While some of the group were admitted to an asylum procedure in Italy, reports indicate that up to 850 people (primarily Egyptians) were summarily transferred to Libya. UNHCR criticised the Italian authorities for carrying out forced returns without adequate assessments of protection needs. At one stage in Lampedusa, 500 people were being detained in a centre designed for 200 people. In Libya, UNHCR was refused permission to check the safety of those who had been forcibly returned from Italy.[19] Earlier interception measures taken by the USA and Australia have had similar consequences.[20]

Carrier sanctions: 'privatising' member states' responsibilities

Carrier sanctions mean that, in effect, part of the responsibility for assessing protection needs has been passed on from EU member states to personnel employed by transport companies. Such persons are unlikely to be trained in refugee law, and are certainly unaccountable for their actions under international law. By 'privatising' their international responsibilities in this way, member states have created a situation where international principles, such as non-refoulement, could be breached on a regular basis.

Under EU legislation, transport companies (airplanes, trains, and lorries) are liable to penalties of €2000 if one of their passengers is refused entry to the EU. In addition, the carriers are expected to assume responsibility for returning such persons to their country of origin or a third country. Where this is not possible, they must 'take charge' of that person and 'find means of onward transportation'.[21] The relevant EU legislation does not ensure non-refoulement. Nor does it provide any access to remedies for those asylum seekers who have been refused permission to travel by the carriers at the point of departure.

Box 4 Eritreans refouled by Malta

In mid-2003, hundreds of Eritrean asylum seekers were rescued at sea by Maltese authorities when their boats were shipwrecked in the Mediterranean Sea. The Eritreans were detained in Malta.

Malta had not yet joined the EU, but, as a State Party to both the 1951 Refugee Convention and the European Convention on Human Rights, it was bound to comply with its obligations under international law.

Of the 400 asylum seekers rescued at sea, 220 were forcibly deported back to Eritrea between September and October 2003. These included those who had not yet lodged a claim and those who had not yet had a chance to appeal against an initial decision. When they arrived back in Asmara, these people were immediately arrested, taken to a military camp, and detained incommunicado and without charge.

There have been numerous reports that these people, viewed as traitors by the Eritrean government, were later tortured while in detention. Thirty of the detainees subsequently managed to escape from detention and made their way to Sudan, where they were granted refugee status and prioritised for resettlement by UNHCR. More than 150 deportees from Malta are still detained in Eritrea. Eritrean authorities have neither acknowledged the detentions nor revealed the whereabouts of the detainees to their families. There are reports that some members of the group were shot by Eritrean security forces while trying to escape to Sudan.[22]

Recommendations

Principles

- A central principle of international law is that of non-refoulement. This means that asylum seekers must not be turned away from EU territory, or prevented from accessing that territory in the first place, without an adequate assessment of their protection needs taking place.
- Responsibility stems from the actions of states, wherever these actions occur. Therefore EU member states' immigration-control measures must be in line with the obligation to uphold the right to seek asylum.

Application

- EU immigration-control measures must contain effective and non-discriminatory safeguards for differentiating between persons in need of international protection and other migrants.
- These measures must include mechanisms to assess the asylum cases of people claiming to need international protection. Such assessments must be carried out by qualified personnel.
- EU policy makers should meet their objective of creating more and appropriate legal migration channels as part of a comprehensive policy on immigration and asylum.

Securing the co-operation of transit countries

Even as the EU has given more and more attention to controlling its borders, policy makers have realised that migration cannot be 'managed' without co-operation with migrants' countries of origin and countries of transit. In pursuing this agenda, policy makers have sought to take advantage of existing agreements and relations. Particular attention has been given to co-operation with countries in regions bordering the EU: those through which migrants from many countries must pass to reach the EU – namely, countries in North Africa and Eastern Europe.

In October 2001 the Belgian Presidency called for a 'mutually beneficial relationship' between the EU and countries of origin and transit, and stated that the tendency to focus relations on migration management (the EU home-affairs agenda), 'rather than on foreign policy and development measures, should be counterbalanced'.[23] This warning has not been heeded, however, and it has become clear that the goal of EU member states in pursuing these partnerships with third countries is less to reduce emigration from countries of origin than to reduce immigration to the EU.

Partnerships for immigration control – at what cost?

When the European Council met in Seville in June 2002, it called for illegal immigration to be accorded higher priority in external policy, and for immigration-policy concerns to be integrated into the Union's relations with third countries. It urged that a 'clause on joint management of migration flows and on compulsory readmission in the event of illegal immigration' should be included in any future co-operation, association, or equivalent agreement which the EU concludes with any country. (That is, agreements on trade, development co-operation, etc.) The Seville Council also called for assessments of relations with third countries which do not co-operate in combating illegal immigration, and suggested that failure to co-operate in this way would 'hamper the establishment of closer relations'.[24]

During the Council meeting, some member states, including the Spanish Presidency, called for a 'negative migration conditionality', i.e. for the EU to reduce development assistance to those third states that failed to co-operate in combating illegal immigration. Indeed, the German Chancellor Gerhard Schröder later commented, 'I would have liked to see more sanctions introduced against unco-operative countries.'[25] While the Council Conclusions that were finally adopted took a more cautious approach and stressed that measures taken against unco-operative countries must not jeopardise development objectives, the Seville Conclusions nevertheless indicated a clear change of focus.

Following the Seville Conclusions, in November 2002 eight countries were identified for intensified EU co-operation on migration management: Albania, China, FR Yugoslavia, Morocco, Russia, Tunisia, Ukraine, and Turkey.[26] The Council also called for co-operation to be initiated with Libya.[27] With the possible exception of China, all of these are key countries of transit for migrants travelling to the EU. The focus is on controlling movement from transit countries to the EU, rather than addressing the movements from countries of origin.

In contrast to the protection-focused conclusions of Tampere, the Seville Council presented partnerships with third countries primarily as tools for achieving short-term and medium-term migration-management goals; the focus was placed on readmission agreements, and on combating illegal immigration to the EU.[28] In the 'road-map' for the follow-up to Seville, for example, not one of the 24 proposed measures addressed the root causes of forced migration to the EU.[29]

The 'Seville Agenda' re-emerged at the Thessaloniki Council in June 2003. Here EU leaders again stressed the need to monitor the activities of third countries in the fight against illegal immigration. The Council called for an evaluation mechanism to be developed. It is not yet clear what will be the practical consequences for a third state found not to be 'adequately co-operating' with the EU in the fight against illegal immigration. Given the context in which these evaluation mechanisms are being developed, however, there is a serious risk that they will emphasise co-operation (or the lack thereof) in measures related to border controls and interception, while third countries' compliance with international refugee and human-rights law will be given far less attention.

Readmission agreements: returns without safeguards?

As part of its general immigration policy, the European Union has drawn up readmission agreements with migrants' countries of origin and transit. These commit countries to accept back (primarily) their nationals who have been living illegally within the EU. This category includes asylum seekers whose claim has been rejected. The aim is to avoid a situation where the removal of illegal migrants from the EU is delayed or even prevented by the refusal of countries of origin to readmit their nationals. So far, the EU has concluded readmission agreements with Hong Kong, Sri Lanka, Russia, Albania, and Macao, and is in negotiations with Morocco, Ukraine, Turkey, Pakistan, China, and Algeria.

Refugees from Sudan could find themselves returned to Morocco even if they only passed through it.

The priority given to readmission agreements has been made explicit in a number of recent documents, including the draft EU Constitution.[30] The Constitution's wording reflects a trend to apply readmission agreements not only to nationals of the countries in question, but also to persons who may have travelled through these countries on their way to the EU. In other words, refugees from Sudan could find themselves returned to Morocco even if they only passed through it. This trend is accompanied by a new emphasis on 'safe third countries' (see Chapter 2) and extra-territorial processing (Chapter 6), and it raises the same concerns of 'chain refoulement' and the shifting of responsibility.

Readmission agreements, if properly worded, *could* provide an additional safety net to ensure that nobody is sent from the EU to a country where his or her life or freedom may be in danger. When concluding such agreements, the EU should take advantage of the opportunity to elicit guarantees that any asylum seekers returned or transferred to the relevant country will be admitted to the receiving state in conditions of safety and dignity; will be provided (in the case of transfers to countries of transit) with full access to a fair and efficient refugee-status determination procedure; and therefore will be effectively protected against refoulement. They must also be treated in accordance with international human-rights standards.[31]

If this is not the case, individuals could be sent to a situation where they will be at risk. In this way, the very existence of readmission agreements could facilitate the breaching of EU member states' international obligations. It is essential, therefore, that the rights of these persons, when sent back to the transit country, are guaranteed in any agreements concluded by the EU. Of course, such guarantees may be meaningless in practice, if the third country regularly breaches norms of international human rights and refugee law. It is therefore crucial that these considerations should influence the EU's choice of countries with which to conclude readmission agreements.

However, this has not been a factor in the EU's decision making to date: it has often sought to conclude readmission agreements/clauses with third countries irrespective of their poor human-rights records. In fact, and in spite of assurances to the contrary by the European Commission,[32] the examples below show that even where the EU has ample evidence of consistent violations of human rights in a third country, this fact rarely influences efforts to conclude readmission agreements with that country. The EU is considering lifting its embargo on arms sales to China. However, on a visit to China in April 2004, the President of the European Commission said that, due to human-rights concerns, it was improbable that the embargo would be lifted in the near future. During the same visit, however, the case for an 'early signing' of the EU–China readmission agreement was urged.[33]

Libya has not yet signed the 1951 Refugee Convention, or an Association Agreement with the EU. There is detailed evidence of consistent violations of human rights in Libya, and considerable gaps in the provision of protection for refugees and asylum seekers. Due to Libya's geographic significance, however, during the Italian Presidency the EU sought increased co-operation with Libya in the field of immigration controls. The EU has also recently negotiated a 'readmission clause' with Syria, which has not signed the 1951 Convention.[34]

Box 5 Readmission agreements with Sri Lanka – premature and without safeguards

In June 2004, the EU signed a Readmission Agreement with Sri Lanka which is expected to go into force in 2005. According to most members of the human-rights community, in the absence of a formal peace accord this arrangement is premature: *'It is irresponsible of government to return a Sri Lankan without a political solution, especially when political killings still occur.'* [35] A senior UN human-rights officer agrees: *'It is still unclear what safeguards there would be within a devolved system, or what recourse people living under the LTTE would have to national institutions.'*

A number of countries, including the UK, Switzerland, and Norway, also have bilateral agreements with the Sri Lankan government to facilitate the return of Sri Lankan nationals who do not have permission to remain on their territories. Between January and April 2004, the UK and Sri Lanka had an 'exchange of diplomatic notes' to re-document Sri Lankans without passports and deemed illegal in the UK.[36] To implement this agreement, the UK funded the IOM to provide reintegration assistance upon request to the returnee. However, not all have a place to return to once they reach Sri Lankan soil. One recent returnee, a failed asylum seeker, stays with his family at his cousin's home in Colombo. His own house, located in Jaffna less than a kilometre outside the High Security Zone, was completely destroyed, and he has no means to rebuild it. Because his return was not affected under the terms of the informal agreement (since his nationality was not in dispute), he is not eligible for reintegration support. The LTTE in particular is highly suspicious of individuals who have been abroad or have lived in government-controlled territories for extended periods of time. According to one man who recently returned to the Vanni from Norway, LTTE cadres visit frequently and question him about his absence – why he left when others stayed, whom he met, and so forth. When he is away, they harass his family and neighbours.[37] There are no formal mechanisms for the monitoring of failed asylum seekers upon their return to Sri Lanka.

European Neighbourhood Policy: more focus on transit countries

With the enlargement of the EU, EU policy makers are keen to include migration and asylum concerns in its relations with its new neighbours. The stated goal of the European Neighbourhood Policy (ENP) is to share the benefits of the EU's 2004 enlargement with neighbouring countries which have no prospects of imminent EU membership. The ENP offers these countries increased political, security, economic, and cultural co-operation, based on 'common values' regarding the rule of law, good governance, respect for human rights, the principles of market economy, and sustainable development. In December 2004, the European Commission approved agreements with countries in Eastern Europe and the southern Mediterranean: Israel, Jordan, Moldova, Morocco, the Palestinian Authority, Tunisia, and Ukraine.[38] After being excluded from the initial stages, Armenia, Azerbaijan, and Georgia will also be offered the prospect of joining the initiative.[39] In addition, joint plans with Egypt, Lebanon, and Algeria are expected to follow in early 2005.[40]

A set of common priorities will be agreed with each partner country, to be incorporated into Action Plans covering a range of policy areas, including political dialogue, development, trade, and justice and home affairs. The priorities set in the Action Plans will also guide the financial support provided by the EU to the relevant countries. Existing financial assistance to these countries will be complemented from 2007 onwards by a new instrument: the European Neighbourhood Instrument.[41]

The March 2003 Communication which first outlined the ENP called on the EU to 'assist in reinforcing the neighbouring countries' efforts to combat illegal migration and to establish efficient mechanisms for returns, especially illegal transit migration'. The document also emphasises the need to conclude readmission agreements with a range of countries in Eastern Europe and North Africa.[42] This emphasis underlines the fact that many ENP countries are transit countries for migrants to Europe. A May 2004 Communication suggests that 'border management is likely to be a priority in most Action Plans'. The Communication makes direct reference to the management of legal migration and implementation of migration plans for the countries of North Africa.[43]

The Commission has stressed that the ENP will build on 'mutual commitment to common values', including respect for the rule of law and human rights. In the May 2004 Communication, however, joint measures to strengthen the protection capacity of the countries in question are not identified as a priority issue. Potential co-operation in the field of immigration-control measures, on the other hand, is discussed in far greater detail. Nowhere is it mentioned that asylum systems in many of the participating countries fall far below international standards. Indeed, as of 1 August 2004, Lebanon and Jordan had acceded to neither the 1951 Convention nor the 1967 Protocol.[44]

Although Libya and Belarus are not included in immediate ENP plans, they are repeatedly referred to as potential future partners of the EU within the ENP framework.[45] Both countries are of concern to EU policy makers, because they are important transit countries for migrants travelling to the EU, and this would appear to be an important motivating factor in the search for closer partnerships. However, there are serious concerns regarding the treatment of refugees and asylum seekers in Libya and Belarus. Numerous organisations have reported cases of arbitrary detention, inadequate asylum procedures, and even refoulement of asylum seekers from these countries.[46] Any attempts to incorporate Belarus and Libya into the ENP must first address these concerns.

Focus on North Africa

North Africa is a particular focus for 'migration management' co-operation initiatives, because many asylum seekers have to travel through countries such as Libya, Tunisia, and Morocco in order to reach Europe. At the bilateral level, in 2004 there were negotiations between Libya and Italy about migration control, including the possibility of setting up processing camps in Libya (see Chapter 6), as well as similar German proposals for Tunisia.

At the same time, the EU funded a project for institution building for asylum in five North African countries: Algeria, Libya, Mauritania, Morocco, and Tunisia.[47] Initial reports suggested that this project aimed to establish reception centres in those countries, which prompted concerns that this could be a first step towards establishing external processing there. UNHCR, which will be implementing these projects, has strongly rejected such claims, however, and has clarified that the projects seek to build or strengthen asylum systems in these countries: 'promoting legislation, training of officials in refugee status determination, assisting NGOs in building their capacities, etc. Reception centres do not feature at all in this project.'[48]
The Italian and German bilateral proposals, however, raise fears that efforts to strengthen (drastically underdeveloped) asylum systems in North Africa may in future be invoked by EU policy makers in order to justify a move towards 'processing in the regions'. These proposals will be discussed in greater detail in Chapter 6.

Recommendations

Principles

- Migration-management concerns must not dominate or dictate EU relationships with third countries. In particular, development co-operation should never be made conditional on co-operation in 'migration management'; and migration-management concerns must not detract from EU action to promote human rights and democratisation in third countries.

Application

- States signing EU Neighbourhood or Readmission agreements, or other EU or bilateral 'migration management' agreements, must guarantee to protect and not to refoule people who are transferred to their territory.

- The EU and its member states should avoid concluding readmission agreements or other 'migration management' agreements with countries which have inadequate asylum systems, which are not signatories to the 1951 Convention, and/or which have poor human-rights records.

- In negotiating readmission agreements, the EU and member states should elicit meaningful guarantees from third countries on the treatment of migrants returned there.
- In implementing the European Neighbourhood Policy (ENP), EU leaders should emphasise not merely migration management, but also the need to strengthen the refugee-protection capacities of the third countries concerned. Those ENP countries that have not acceded to the 1951 Convention, and/or to other major human-rights instruments, should be encouraged to do so.
- EU leaders and third countries should commit themselves to monitoring and evaluating the impact of migration-management activities on the protection of vulnerable people, in particular the impact on returned asylum seekers.

Regions of origin (I): new approaches to orderly entry 5

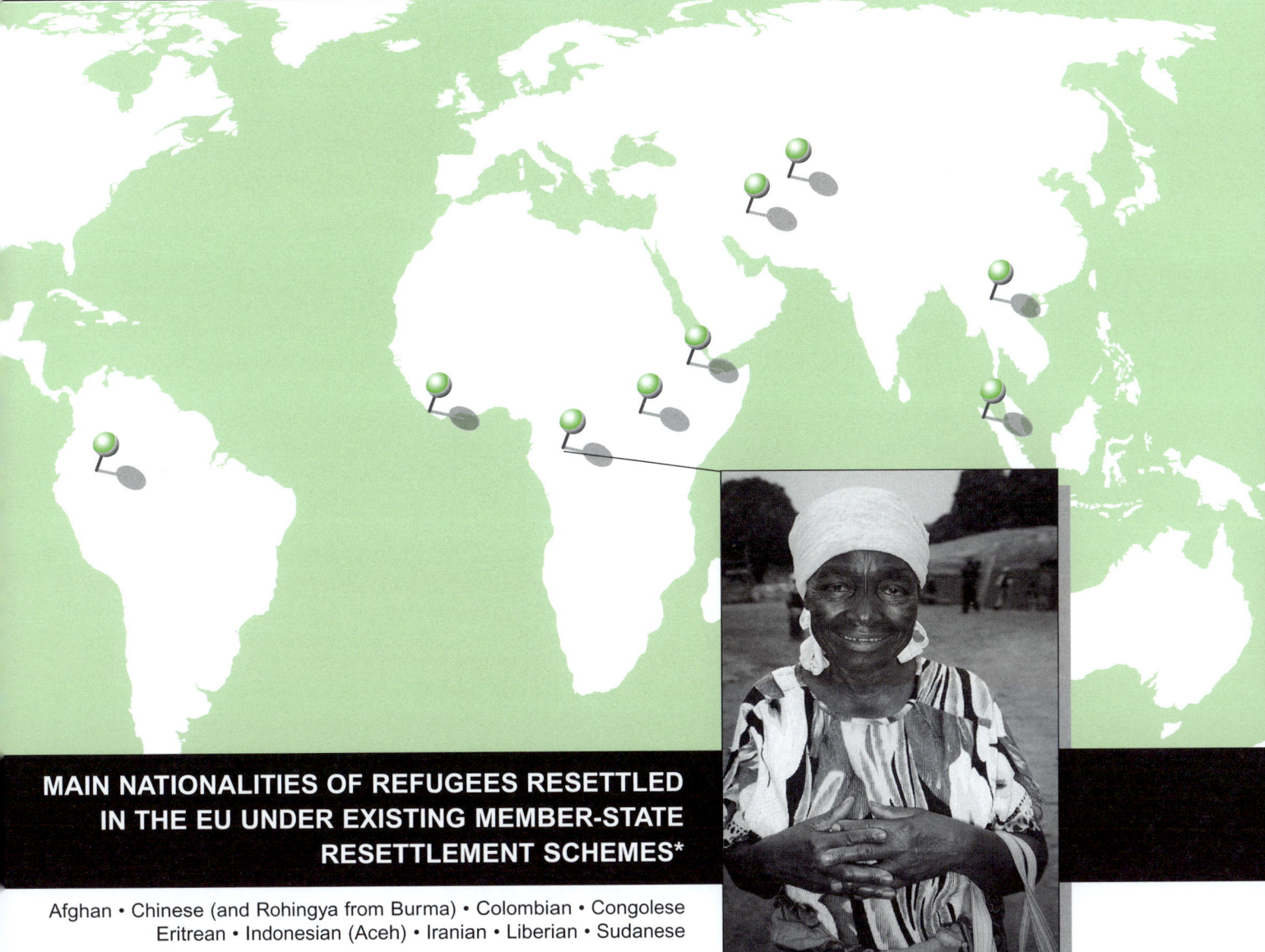

MAIN NATIONALITIES OF REFUGEES RESETTLED IN THE EU UNDER EXISTING MEMBER-STATE RESETTLEMENT SCHEMES*

Afghan • Chinese (and Rohingya from Burma) • Colombian • Congolese
Eritrean • Indonesian (Aceh) • Iranian • Liberian • Sudanese

Kigoma transit centre, Tanzania, 2004: a Congolese refugee selected for resettlement from Lugufu camp
© Jessica Schultz

5
Regions of origin (I):
new approaches to orderly entry

> *... resettlement programmes, if properly managed and adequately resourced, and sensibly publicised by Member States and the EU, can assist in the development of a public understanding of refugees and their reasons for seeking protection in the countries receiving those refugees and others in need of international protection and in enhancing the efficiency of the EU in combating human trafficking.*
>
> European Parliament, Committee on Civil Liberties, Justice and Home Affairs [1]

At the same time as raising barriers against asylum seekers in general, EU governments are considering ways to provide safe passage to the EU for a select number of refugees, direct from their regions of origin. These proposed antidotes to the 'access dilemma' take the form of formal 'resettlement' schemes and 'protected entry procedures', under the aegis of a 'regional task force'. At this stage neither scheme is beyond the proposal stage. Unfortunately, neither seems to be backed by a level of resources and political will equivalent to that which supports border controls and interception measures.

The majority of the world's refugees are hosted in countries in their regions of origin, with inadequate provision, continued risks, and no prospect of a durable solution. The proposed schemes could represent a necessary lifeline for individual refugees in these situations, as well as a sharing of responsibility with the often poor and overburdened host countries.

However, resettlement and Protected Entry Procedures are also presented by the EU as means of 'managing migration' and achieving 'orderly entry' of the currently 'disorderly' flow of asylum seekers to the EU. This is a misconception, because these selective protection tools can only complement the individual right to claim asylum. Even if these proposals are implemented and well resourced, such 'orderly arrival schemes' cannot be a substitute for allowing 'spontaneously arriving' asylum seekers to obtain asylum in the EU.

Resettlement: not a substitute for asylum

Resettlement involves selecting refugees who have continuing needs for protection in their country of first asylum (usually a country in their region of origin) and transferring them to a third country which has agreed to grant them permanent residence status. A number of countries operate resettlement schemes and select refugees for resettlement, according to varying criteria. Cases are often identified by UNHCR, and other international organisations and NGOs are involved in selection and processing. The USA, for example, regularly carries out resettlement through the Joint Voluntary Agency (JVA), a group of agencies which performs a variety of tasks related to the processing of resettlement applications. It has been suggested that a similar system could usefully be applied if the EU began operating resettlement schemes on a larger scale.[2]

Resettlement is an important and welcome component of the global refugee-protection regime, because it offers protection and a durable solution for individuals in need, and is an active gesture of international solidarity with countries of first asylum. An EU resettlement scheme would be a positive development, offering a safe solution for the individuals selected for it. If conducted on a significant and strategic scale, it could help to resolve protracted refugee situations. In the longer term, the targeted use of resettlement could increase the protection capacity of countries in regions of origin.

However, resettling refugees from regions of origin does not obviate the legal and humanitarian responsibility of states to grant asylum to persons in need of international protection who arrive 'spontaneously' on their territory or at their borders. As UNHCR has commented:

> *Resettlement and asylum are two distinct and separate possibilities. It is therefore critical to the integrity of the international protection system that resettlement processing and the promotion of asylum are pursued in tandem, and not used to work against each other [..] Resettlement must continue to function as a complement to other protection activities and durable solutions. It is not a substitute for the right to seek and enjoy asylum.* [3]

Resettlement therefore should not and cannot end spontaneous arrivals, as often claimed by EU proponents. The Commission has argued that 'if access to protection can be offered, as quickly as possible and as close to the needs as possible of those concerned and which facilitated a safe and legal avenue to protection in the EU, then there would be no need for those in need of protection to pay traffickers for a dangerous and illegal journey to the EU'.[4]

There is minimal evidence to support this claim. No country which carries out resettlement in significant numbers has seen a marked drop in the numbers of 'spontaneous arrivals' as a direct consequence of resettlement schemes.[5] As one asylum expert notes, it is also a matter of concern that moves towards an EU resettlement scheme could be used in the future to justify a policy change which discriminates against spontaneous arrivals on the groundless premise 'that there is no longer a necessity for asylum-seekers to enter illegally or under false pretences because of the existence of an alternative "gateway", although in reality this is small and selective'.[6]

Distinguishing between 'legitimate' resettled refugees and 'illegitimate' asylum seekers could lead to a two-tier system of rights for refugees in the EU. This has already occurred in Australia, which accepts resettled refugees *in place of* granting asylum to 'spontaneous arrivals' and accords lesser rights to the latter, even if they have been accepted as 'Convention refugees'.[7]

Moves towards an EU Resettlement Programme

Resettlement to Europe is not a new phenomenon. In total, seven EU member states currently operate resettlement programmes. The numbers of refugees resettled to the EU remains small, however. While the USA resettles on average 80,000–120,000 refugees each year, the combined number for EU member states remains around 4000–5000 refugees per year.[8] Until recently, many member states appeared reluctant to commit themselves to resettling refugees on a regular basis, or to establish EU-wide resettlement programmes to co-ordinate such action.

Recently, however, there has been interest in creating an EU resettlement scheme as part of a drive to 'ensure more orderly and managed entry in the EU of persons in need of international protection'.[9] According to proposals, there would be a general EU procedural framework, which would serve as the basis for situation-specific schemes targeting particular refugee caseloads. UNHCR would play a role in selecting and referring refugees for resettlement.[10]

While the USA resettles on average 80,000–120,000 refugees each year, the combined number for EU member states remains around 4000–5000.

It is proposed that those eligible for resettlement would include both 'Convention refugees' and those who fall outside the 1951 Convention but are found to be in need of 'subsidiary protection status'. The EU would also take some responsibility for vulnerable groups of refugees, and those facing integration difficulties in the third country concerned. Importantly, this would complement US, Canadian, and Australian resettlement schemes, which do not always focus on vulnerability,[11] but on selecting those refugees who demonstrate the best prospect of integration into their new country.

There is increasing interest in resettlement, and a Council conclusion on durable solutions recommended the creation of an EU resettlement programme. However, as yet there appears to be little political will to establish binding EU instruments on resettlement. Instead, the emphasis is on EU co-ordination and flexible participation, by way of financial assistance or actual physical resettlement, and the idea of 'targets rather than quotas or ceilings' for member states.[12] It appears that selection criteria for resettlement will initially be left to member states; after a period there will be discussions on which practices work best, and only in the long term is a common EU resettlement system likely.

A June 2004 Communication suggests that one advantage of resettlement is that orderly and managed entry of refugees would allow member states to anticipate the arrival of persons determined to be in need of international protection. This is seen as advantageous in terms of planning (for housing, financial impacts, and integration programmes). It is also suggested that resettling refugees whose identity and history have been screened would be 'preferable from a security perspective'.[13]

This is certainly important, but it must not risk protracting the time between selection and departure. Resettlement is intended to help refugees who are not being effectively protected in their country of asylum; the longer it takes to process resettlement applications, the longer the refugee must remain in a potentially insecure environment. Extended delays will increase the chances of a refugee's human rights being violated in his or her country of first asylum. This could force some refugees to seek other means to escape this insecure environment – i.e. by way of traffickers and smugglers. At present, stringent pre-departure requirements mean that, from the time of submission of the resettlement dossier to the date of departure, it may take ten months for a refugee to be resettled to the USA, Canada, or Australia.[14] In some cases, increased security constraints have left some resettlement applicants in limbo for up to four years. If an EU resettlement scheme is to be an effective protection tool, these extended delays must be avoided.

Because there are well-established resettlement schemes in existence across the world, there are plenty of examples to illustrate how the various actors – governments, UNHCR, and NGOs – can work together to select the most vulnerable for resettlement. Co-operation at the field level, as well as in Brussels, is crucial if resettlement schemes are to respond effectively to the protection needs of individuals and groups in a variety of situations.

Box 6 Resettlement of Congolese from Tanzania

'I spend a lot of time counselling people about resettlement and reassuring them that no one will force them back [home].'

The EU's resettlement proposals are currently driven by a call for 'orderly entry' into the EU. However, an assessment of refugee realities, grounded in field-based knowledge, would help to ensure that the proposals accord with the real needs of refugees, and that they take better account of the operational implications. Our research in the camps in western Tanzania revealed two issues central to operating an effective resettlement scheme: the need to prioritise the most vulnerable people, and the need for adequate resources.

Fair, transparent, and needs-based resettlement programmes are demanding to implement anywhere in the world. Tanzania is no exception. Unlike Kenya, where major operations have moved thousands of Sudanese 'Lost Boys' and Somali Bantus to new lives in the United States, Tanzania has remained a low-profile source of resettlement referrals. In 2003, for example, the cases of only 1281 individuals were submitted by UNHCR to resettlement governments for consideration.[15] Many belonged to the so-called 'ex-Kigwa' caseload, consisting of Congolese who came to Tanzania in 1969, achieved self-sufficiency in a settlement known as Kigwa, and then moved to refugee camps in 1998, when Kigwa was closed by the authorities. Individual referrals included 'women-at-risk', Congolese with 'Tutsi' physical features (suspected of having allegiance to Rwanda), and couples in ethnically mixed marriages.

Without a safe haven: women at risk

Tanzanian authorities frequently allege that Northern countries choose to resettle 'the healthy, brainy' refugees who are more likely to integrate easily.[16] However, resettlement also provides a purely humanitarian solution for many survivors of sexual violence – most of whom lack language skills or professional skills. In Tanzania, 'women at risk' constitute a priority category of referrals for UNHCR.

Sexual violence was perpetrated as a weapon of war by all of the warring factions in the Congo, including the Rwandan Interhamwe, the Rassemblement Congolais pour la Démocratie (RCD), Mai Mai militia, and the Burundian rebels.[17] Combatants and non-combatants alike continue to perpetrate sexual violence with impunity in eastern regions of the Democratic Republic of Congo (DRC). Although the precise prevalence of sexual violence is unknown, in Baraka, where many refugees in Tanzania originate, Médecins Sans Frontières (MSF) treated more than 550 cases of sexual violence between August 2003 and January 2004. It estimates that hundreds, if not thousands, have been unable to access help.[18]

Victims range in age from 20-month-old babies to 80-year-old women. Moreover, for survivors of past abuse, medical, psychosocial, and socio-economic effects linger, as MSF reports in its publication 'I Have No Joy'. One Congolese woman in Ituri district described the aftermath of her own rape: '*When the soldiers came into the house they said to my husband, "We want to rape your wife". At first he said "no", but they threatened to kill him. After they had raped me, my husband shouted bad words at me and blamed me for bringing this shame. He then threw me out of the house.*' [19]

In the camps, the consequences for refugee survivors of sexual violence can be dire. As one Congolese man explained, rape '*is a curse. In our tribe a woman who's been raped is like a prostitute.*' Service providers report that women raped during flight are commonly cast out from family homes once they reach Tanzania. The confined conditions of the camps simply reinforce the social exclusion that survivors too often suffer.

Resourcing resettlement in Tanzania

Resettlement poses numerous challenges for the UNHCR in Tanzania. First of all, resettlement activities consume a huge volume of staff resources. The Deputy Representative based in Dar es Salaam estimates that 50–70 per cent of the protection team's time is spent on resettlement. Two senior protection posts were recently abolished in Tanzania, shifting an even greater burden on to junior staff. Compounding the administrative problems is the fact that implementing partners have limited experience in identifying cases that meet resettlement criteria.

One UNHCR staff member also noted that resettlement can detract from other protection interventions: '*Resettlement [activities have] made it much more difficult to identify legitimate protection cases. When I come to the camp, most people are eager to convince me that they need to leave the country. I spend a lot of time counselling people about resettlement and reassuring them that no one will force them back [home].*'

A third challenge is that UNHCR lacks detailed data about the population whom it assists. This makes it difficult to cross-check individual cases or undertake larger-scale resettlement. UNHCR only recently launched a comprehensive refugee-registration exercise in the Lugufu camps. This means that critical information (on aspects such as ethnicity) was not collected until 2004 – after residents had discerned certain patterns in resettlement processing. For example, since many Congolese with 'Tutsi' physical features go straight to Mkugwa, popularly known as a 'protection camp' (and therefore a source of resettlement referrals), many people in Lugufu now insist that they, too, have Tutsi ancestry. Field officers cannot easily assess these claims. Furthermore, the renewed emphasis on resettlement by staff at headquarters means that UNHCR field offices face pressure to process people on a group basis. Such groups might share common protection problems or a unique flight history, or they might have particularly limited prospects of finding another solution. In Tanzania, for example, many Burundian farmers have remained in exile for more than three decades and no longer own land at home. Without adequate information it is impossible to identify individuals who fit the relevant criteria.

Despite these challenges, UNHCR expects that the number of referrals from Tanzania in 2004 will double those made in 2003.[20] In addition to its established focus on women-at-risk and other protection cases, it is profiling other refugees with particularly compelling needs for a durable solution.

Protected Entry Procedures

Another 'orderly entry' proposal involves 'protected entry procedures': a kind of humanitarian visa. At present, people fleeing persecution are often caught in the trap of being unable to apply for a visa to travel legally, partly because of their fear of approaching authorities and partly because of harsh visa restrictions imposed by EU countries. For example, at a time when perceived repression by authorities began forcing some Zimbabwean nationals to seek asylum in the EU, the UK and Ireland swiftly imposed visa restrictions on all Zimbabweans, automatically obstructing the access of many persons in need of international protection.[21]

A protected entry procedure (PEP) would allow a person who wished to claim asylum in an EU country to approach an embassy, rather than having to risk the dangerous journey to the country itself. The embassy, either in the asylum seeker's home country or in a neighbouring country, could assess their claim. If officials decided that the person might need protection, they would grant an entry document so that he or she could travel legally and safely.

Like resettlement, PEPs demand to be based on sound knowledge and strong safeguards. With those provisos, 'humanitarian visas' could represent a lifeline of safe passage for vulnerable people in need of protection. They would not guarantee to 'manage migration', but, operated in conjunction with a fair scheme for spontaneous arrivals, they could form an important element of a comprehensive asylum system.

Some European countries, including Austria, France, the Netherlands, Spain, and the UK, have already operated schemes like these – often in an *ad hoc* and informal manner and affecting only a few asylum seekers. Denmark abolished its PEP procedures in 2002, as did the Netherlands more recently, and Austria has taken steps to do likewise. Outside the EU, Switzerland has long operated PEPs on a formal basis. In addition, six other member states do allow informal access in exceptional cases: Belgium, Germany, Ireland, Italy, Luxembourg, and Portugal.[22]

The scale of the impact of these procedures is limited, due to both their *ad hoc* nature and the reluctance of states to publicise these channels widely, for fear of being overwhelmed by applications. The European Commission has presented the creation of a harmonised PEP scheme as one way of making this safety-valve more effective.[23] A 2003 feasibility study argued that PEPs represent 'the most adequate response to the challenge of reconciling migration control objectives with the obligation of protecting refugees'.[24]

'Humanitarian visas' could represent a lifeline of safe passage for vulnerable people in need of protection.

However, there has been minimal political will on the part of member states to take these recommendations forward. Member states showed far less enthusiasm for PEPs than for increased activity in the field of resettlement, expressing concern that their embassies would lack the resources to deal with large numbers of applications from protection seekers.[25] EU-level PEPs are not therefore under active consideration at present. Instead, the June 2004 Communication suggests that PEPs could be employed as an 'emergency strand' of wider resettlement action in specific circumstances, as appropriate. Refugee-status determination would take place in the EU, after an initial screening process (presumably in the non-EU country where the application was made), for those with urgent protection needs.[26] It is regrettable that there has been no political will to consider the merits of PEPs, and that the trend is towards abolishing rather than harmonising the schemes of individual member states.

Box 7 Protected Entry Procedures in practice: the Swiss Embassy in Sri Lanka

People facing persecution in Sri Lanka frequently have no choice but to embark on a risky, costly journey to obtain protection in another country. 'Agents', or people smugglers, procure false passports and arrange transport by air or, more dangerously, by sea – all for around $5000. Deaths in the back of lorries or on un-seaworthy boats are not uncommon. Often refugees travel from Sri Lanka to Italy through the Suez Canal, or even through Somalia.[27] From Italy, they make an overland journey into western Europe.

Switzerland operates a protected-entry programme which provides a safe, legal alternative for people deemed to have a legitimate claim to asylum. There are approximately 40,000 Sri Lankan nationals living in Switzerland, most with legal status of some kind. Each year, around 500 persons apply for asylum – 100 of whom do not leave their country to do so.[28] Although other embassies may accept emergency applicants on a case-by-case basis, the Swiss embassy had, until August 2004, a professional attaché from the Ministry of Justice and Police dedicated solely to hearing and investigating claims in Sri Lanka. After checking the facts of an applicant's story, the attaché decided whether he or she should travel to Switzerland for a formal hearing, where the applicant's case would be judged on its merits by the Swiss Office of Refugees.

Before the ceasefire was signed, the embassy received 300 claims a year and accepted approximately 10 per cent of them. From mid-2003 through mid-2004, only 100 claims were made, and the acceptance rate remained constant. In addition, approximately 400 persons filed a claim directly in Switzerland. Although women comprised nearly half of all asylum seekers, men were the primary applicants in ninety per cent of the cases.

According to the embassy attaché, most successful cases were referred by a mandated protection agency such as the ICRC, UNICEF, or UNHCR. They mainly involved Tamils who were either political opponents of the LTTE or escapees or dissenters from the north-east, whom the LTTE considered to be traitors. For those people, opportunities for protection on the island have diminished over the past several years. There is currently only one place where runaways can receive assistance: at the Ministry for Youth and Sports in Jaffna. Since the LTTE can and do travel around the country, there is no 'internal flight alternative' for such individuals.

Because the demand for asylum has declined since the ceasefire, the Swiss government decided to discontinue the dedicated post in 2004. Visa officers will assume the responsibility for recommending travel documents, although obviously the expertise and dedicated resources will diminish.

The Protected Entry Procedure was only one element of the Swiss government's migration-management programme. In conjunction with its readmission arrangement with the Sri Lankan authorities, the embassy assists returnees on a case-by-case basis through the provision of a cash grant and transportation back to villages of origin. It also provides funds to the Home for Human Rights to help returnees to reclaim the money that they earned abroad. About 150 persons returned in 2003. The Ministry of Justice and Police also controls special funds for 'structural assistance' in Sri Lanka, aimed at mitigating the need to migrate. In 2003, a total of 800,000 Swiss Francs was spent on building schools in Jaffna, and a Swiss expert was seconded to the Ministry of Education to advise on how to increase rural children's access to education. This budget line falls under the Swiss Development Co-operation, part of the Ministry of Foreign Affairs. Sri Lanka is not the only example of explicitly linked programmes. In Kosovo, the Ministry of Justice made decisions regarding approximately three-quarters of the budget of the Ministry of Foreign Affairs.

Increased EU presence in the regions

With the increasing focus on activities overseas in the field of 'migration management' and 'orderly entry', the EU has investigated ways of extending its presence in the countries concerned, to implement these schemes. There are proposals for the EU to increase its presence in a specific region of origin, with more staff and resources working specifically on asylum and migration-related issues. Such an EU regional body could ensure greater efficiency and more responsive activities in regions of origin, and could provide a platform for dialogue with the host countries and stakeholders. However, there is also the risk that it could add a layer of bureaucracy and be dominated by a 'migration management' agenda.

A number of models have been proposed by experts. As a long-term objective, the EU could increase its presence by, for example, expanding an existing sub-section of an existing EU Delegation, which would focus specifically on asylum and immigration matters (i.e. an 'EU Regional Node' on asylum and immigration). One proposed short-term alternative could be to create EU 'Regional Task Forces' to co-ordinate EU activities in a given context, for example in a crisis situation or as part of a comprehensive approach to a specific refugee situation. In each case, the function of these bodies would be to facilitate the collecting and sharing of information and improve decision making on asylum-related issues. Other suggestions have focused on EU bodies to support an EU resettlement scheme – a 'European Clearing System for Resettlement' (ECSR);[29] while some NGOs are currently considering the idea of European Refugee Co-ordinators (ERCs) in regions of origin.

The European Commission has itself suggested the formation of an EU Regional Task Force. Its exact function and form have yet to be clarified, but it would essentially be a joint regional focal point to advise and operate the various asylum/migration-related activities in the region.[30] This kind of decentralisation of EU decision making would be consistent with recent developments within the European Commission's External Relations Directorate, where the EU Delegations are being given more and more power to implement policies within their region. Because the Commission linked this idea to the PEPS proposal, however, the absence of political will for PEPs now means that the idea of EU RTFs / regional nodes is not high on the political agenda for EU policy makers.

If managed in a well-resourced and well-planned manner, increased EU presence in regions of origin could be an opportunity to ensure that EU migration-management policy is based on an accurate understanding of protection needs. If well co-ordinated and given a sufficient level of decision-making power, it would not amount to an extra layer of bureaucracy; rather, it would be a co-ordinated means of supplying information about refugee realities to Brussels and member states. It could be a means to improve the sharing of current and detailed information on countries of transit and regions and countries of origin. In this way, greater regional presence could inform asylum procedures within the EU (as part of the CEAS). It could provide a forum for direct consultation with organisations which have direct understanding of conditions and protection needs in regions of origin.

At present, missions by resettlement countries occur infrequently and are not responsive to demand. As a result, vulnerable refugees often have to wait for extended periods in an insecure environment until the next resettlement mission arrives in that region. These delays could be

Vulnerable refugees often have to wait for extended periods in an insecure environment until the next resettlement mission arrives in that region.

greatly reduced, decisions could be taken much quicker, and pre-departure security checks and orientation exercises could be carried out more easily, if the EU had a body which was permanently based in that region, specifically mandated to make these decisions and carry out these tasks. An EU regional body focusing on asylum and immigration could support EU Delegations to monitor the impact of EU policies, disseminate information on legal migration routes, and serve as a focal point for dialogue with governments in regions of origin. The failure to undertake this kind of dialogue with third countries has already undermined EU initiatives in the field of asylum and migration (as with the High Level Working Group: see Chapter 7).

Despite this potential, given the general direction of EU asylum policies over the past decade, it is worth considering whether greater regional presence would function as 'migration management' outposts and so in practice *increase* the obstacles for those seeking protection in the EU. In other words, would an EU regional body merely serve to strengthen Fortress Europe, rather than counter-balance it? Furthermore, if an EU regional body is to be effective, it is crucial that the body is given some decision-making power. Much of the rationale behind increasing regional presence would disappear if the body was forced to defer to Brussels before making all decisions. Finally, as this would be a multilateral initiative, and one which would be operated beyond EU territory, the accountability of each member state under international law might become unclear.[31] This lack of clarity could allow some member states to evade their responsibilities to refugees.

Recommendations

Principles

- EU resettlement schemes or other 'orderly entry' measures must be complementary to, not a replacement for, a full and fair system for dealing with spontaneous arrivals of asylum seekers on EU territory. Resettlement must be viewed as a tool for providing international protection and durable solutions for selected refugees, and not as a tool of migration management. Any distinctions between 'good' resettled refugees and 'bad' spontaneous arrivals must be avoided, in rhetoric and in practice.
- Within this context, member states should be encouraged to expand their resettlement activity; first within a guiding EU framework, and subsequently as part of a more coherent EU-wide resettlement scheme.

Application

- EU Member States should continue the European tradition of conducting resettlement on the basis of vulnerability and protection needs, not solely on prospects for integration.
- The implementation of resettlement schemes should be properly resourced, in order to operate effectively and not detract from protection activities. EU member states should draw on the experience and knowledge of UNHCR and NGOs that operate resettlement schemes.
- If member states are unwilling to operate PEPs, they should be encouraged not to place obstructive visa restrictions on nationals from countries where human-rights violations are widespread.

Regions of origin (II): enhancing protection or exporting asylum? 6

COUNTRIES / REGIONS REPORTED DURING 2003/4 TO BE UNDER CONSIDERATION BY EU MEMBER STATES AS POSSIBLE SITES FOR 'PROTECTION IN THE REGIONS' INITIATIVES

Balkans • Benin • Burkina Faso • Kenya
Somalia • South Africa • Tanzania • Ukraine

Kigoma, Tanzania, 2004: refugees who have chosen to return to the Democratic Republic of Congo, despite uncertainties about their future there
© Jessica Schultz

6
Regions of origin (II): enhancing protection or exporting asylum?

> *'The problems of Africa should be solved with the help of Europe in Africa, they cannot be solved in Europe.'*
> Otto Schilly, German Minister for Home Affairs, calling for processing camps in Tunisia [1]
>
> *The reception of refugees in the region does not absolve the Member states of the European Union from the duties which they have as the asylum seekers' host countries under the international Conventions [...] keeping refugees in peripheral countries must not become a long-term solution.*
> European Parliament, December 2000 [2]

While resettlement offers safe passage to the EU for a select number of refugees, several EU initiatives have been proposed to ensure that more refugees remain in their countries of first asylum. These initiatives follow two main themes: improving protection standards in the regions of origin so that refugees are not forced to move on, and moving European asylum-processing systems to regions of origin and transit. Once again, these areas are at the proposals stage, although pilot projects and bilateral initiatives are imminent. While the protection agenda is more positive than the processing agenda, both have been characterised by migration-management imperatives, lack of transparency and clarity, and failure to take into account the realities of the refugee situations in which they aim to intervene.

The majority of the world's refugees remain in the first country that they reach in their regions of origin. However, many feel forced to move on because they are receiving inadequate protection. The push and pull factors which lead people to make this onward journey are diverse and situation-specific. EU policy makers frequently emphasise the need to address these 'secondary movements' of people to Europe. Given the range of immigration controls discussed above, secondary movements to the EU tend to be 'irregular' and 'unmanaged' – that is, people enter EU territory without express legal permission, often by way of people smugglers and traffickers. Limiting secondary movements by creating conditions where refugees will stay contained in the first country that they reach is seen by EU policy makers as a way of 'managing migration' to the EU.

Processing asylum applications outside the EU: the UK's 'New Vision'

One side of the debate has focused on ways for EU member states to process asylum applications outside the European Union, so that a large part – if not all – of the domestic asylum system is transferred overseas. Unlike Protected Entry Procedures, which would cater for exceptional cases and grant access to the EU, recent discussions on 'extra-territorial processing' have explored ways of transferring *en masse* those who *do* manage to reach the EU, sending them back to processing centres in their regions of origin. In this way, some member states have come to see 'processing in the region' and 'protection in the region' as two sides of the same 'migration management' coin.

Recent debates on this subject were catalysed by a letter from the UK to the Presidency of the European Union on 10 March 2003.[3] The UK presented a 'New Vision' of a protection regime based on two elements: 'transit processing centres' (TPCs) and 'regional protection areas' (RPAs).

In the short term, it proposed that applicants for asylum within the EU would be sent to TPCs, closed centres or camps to be located outside the borders of the EU, along major transit routes. Those whose claims were approved would be eligible for resettlement to the EU on a 'burden-sharing' basis. The UK acknowledged that the TPCs must not expose people to cruel and inhuman treatment, as prohibited under the European Convention on Human Rights.[4]

In the long term, the UK proposed improving protection conditions in regions of origin. This would include measures to address root causes of forced migration, to develop managed resettlement programmes, and to establish RPAs in regions of origin. Unsuccessful asylum applicants could be returned, by the EU, to an RPA in their region of origin. Here they would receive 'temporary support until conditions allowed for voluntary returns' to their country of origin. The UK emphasised the need to conclude readmission agreements with countries in regions of origin, to facilitate these returns.

The UK letter and subsequent versions of the 'New Vision' were characterised more by the questions that they raised than by the solutions that they offered. Furnished with no geographical or logistical details, and based on no evident understanding of the realities faced by refugees or their hosts, they raised a host of fundamental questions with international implications of a legal, moral, and practical nature.[5] Some of the countries suggested for hosting TPCs under the plan were Albania, Croatia, Iran, Morocco, Romania, Russia, northern Somalia, Turkey, and Ukraine. Almost all of these countries have records of violating the rights of asylum seekers, refugees, and migrants.[6]

The proposed shifting of the burden of caring for Europe's refugees on to poor countries which could not guarantee their safety provoked opposition from many quarters,[7] including the European Parliament, which

> *considers that centres for the holding of would-be migrants in the country of final transit have no place in the consideration of durable solutions in the region, nor in offering sanctuary to those in need of international protection; indeed believes that while such centres may seem to provide a short-term solution to certain migratory pressures they raise many questions about the ability to meet international obligations in terms of human rights, not least due to the very poor human rights records of the regimes of many of those transit countries.*[8]

Consideration of the TPC element of the UK plan was deferred indefinitely and, after a cautious Communication from the Commission in June 2003,[9] the 'New Vision' received an unenthusiastic response from the European Council at Thessaloniki. In Brussels it emerged that the Netherlands, Denmark, Italy, and Spain had given a 'cautious welcome' to the UK's proposal, whereas Germany and Sweden, in particular, had significant reservations. The UK decided to pursue its ideas on a bilateral basis with some other interested states, including Tanzania and South Africa. These negotiations have been conducted at a highly confidential diplomatic level, and although there have been reports that Tanzania had rejected the UK proposals, the current terms and progress of negotiations is not known.

Regional Protection Programmes: strengthening the protection capacity of refugees' region of origin

Proposals for Regional Protection Programmes involve the provision of financial and technical assistance and resources to third countries to assist them to provide better protection (legal, physical, and material) to refugees in that country. More than 70 per cent of the world's refugees are currently hosted in developing countries, many in 'protracted refugee situations'.[10] EU action to improve conditions for refugees in developing countries has been presented, partly, as a way to correct this imbalance. It is presented as a solution to the plight of refugees in protracted situations, a gesture of solidarity with the overburdened host countries, and a capacity-building measure to help these countries to become 'robust providers of effective protection'.[11] The basic logic underlying recent EU policy documents is that if protection conditions in regions of origin can be improved, there will be no need for refugees to move beyond these regions and seek asylum in the EU.

Reflecting the apparent shift in emphasis in the June 2003 Communication from processing to protection, the Thessaloniki European Council asked the European Commission to further explore 'ways and means to enhance the protection capacity of regions of origin'. The Conclusions made no explicit reference to processing centres, either within or outside the borders of the EU, but did request the Commission to examine ways to speed up the processing of applicants who did not have a genuine asylum claim.[12]

In response, the Commission's June 2004 Communication, 'on Orderly Entry and Durable Solutions',[13] acknowledges that standards of refugee protection encompass all stages of a refugee situation, from initial reception and status determination, through 'comprehensive protection', to the provision of a Durable Solution. It calls for a 'coordinated and systematic approach' by the EU to strengthen the protection capacity of third countries at each stage.

Along with 'migration management', 'effective protection' is perhaps the most widely used term in current debates on EU asylum. It is cited as an end-goal for interventions in regions of origin and a baseline for conditions in processing centres. According to UNHCR, 'effective protection' is the implementation of the full set of human rights and refugee rights to which refugees are entitled:

> It is the link between observance of Convention obligations, human rights observance, burden-sharing and asylum. It is both the centre and the foundation of a much needed multi-lateral approach to refugee protection [...] Why add 'effective' to the notion of protection? It is in practice and in observance that international standards are transformed from rhetoric into reality.[14]

However, in the absence of a universally accepted definition of 'effective protection', it has become an increasingly politicised term in the 'internationalised asylum' debate, with some states choosing a minimal interpretation which excludes many of the elements necessary for the full protection of refugees. As a result of this politicisation, UNHCR has chosen to abandon the term 'effective', opting instead for 'quality' protection. In the words of the Director for international protection:

> *As we see it, there is a danger in allowing the debate about who is responsible for an asylum seeker to determine the meaning of this term 'effective protection'. We fear the result will be consensus around the lowest common denominator definition.*[15]

Whatever the adjective used to describe protection, it is clear that refugee protection involves putting into practice the full set of rights established in the 1951 Convention and in the international human-rights instruments.

As we have seen in Chapter 3, even the EU's own asylum Directives fall far short of guaranteeing international standards to asylum seekers and refugees arriving in the EU. The June 2004 Communication[16] presents the Common European Asylum System (CEAS) as the basis for standards of 'effective protection' in regions of origin. However, this could result in similar deficiencies being reproduced outside the EU: in other words, EU policies could have a 'negative export value'. Achieving appropriate standards on EU territory must be the prerequisite for extra-territorial actions.

Box 8 Lessons from Lugufu: what makes protection effective?

'If you want to move, you have to escape. If you are caught, you have a problem. Sometimes you have to chop wood, dig toilets, or cut trees for the police. Or they can ask for a bribe. If you can't pay, you'll be brought to the prison in town. There are cases of people staying there for even two years without their case being heard.'

No matter how policy makers ultimately define effective protection, the true test is people's actual sense of security and well-being in a specific refugee context. In Tanzania, gaps in effective protection are illustrated by the flow of refugees returning to the DRC, despite the lack of assistance and safety at home.

From January to August 2004, approximately 1450 Congolese registered with UNHCR to return home.[17] However, it is likely that the actual numbers are much higher, as most refugees who return choose to do so without informing the authorities. The lack of knowledge about what awaits them does not seem to dissuade these returnees. In August 2004, for example, around 100 people officially returned to Bukavu, despite the well-publicised massacre that took place two months earlier.[18]

A 39-year-old woman, one of 64 Congolese waiting in a transit centre for a boat to return home, explained to us: *'I came to Tanzania in 1996 with four children after my husband and three other children were killed. I thought my situation would be better in Tanzania, but the conditions here are so bad. So I'm going home to see whether I can restart my life. I paid for my ticket here from my daughter's bride price (dowry). For me, it's better to die from a bullet than to die from hunger.'*

According to Congolese refugees interviewed for this study, the main push factors are the host government's encampment policy, which denies refugees opportunities to earn an independent income; the negative attitudes of local and national officials, who publicly blame refugees for problems ranging from high crime rates to environmental destruction; inadequate food rations; and bleak prospects for a durable solution through local integration or third-country resettlement.

Congolese refugees reside primarily in three of the 13 refugee camps in north-west Tanzania: Nyarugusu, and Lugufu I and II. As of August 2004, there were 58,504 people (28,464 males and 30,400 females) living in Lugufu I camp, and 34,541 people (17,415 males and 17,126 females) living in Lugufu II.[19]

During our interviews in Lugufu camp, five major gaps in protection provision became evident: access to status determination, freedom of movement, assistance and self-sufficiency, access to durable solutions, and protection of vulnerable groups. Living in these conditions meant an existence without safety and dignity for the refugees. The lessons from Lugufu illustrate the scale of the action and investment needed if EU Regional Protection Programmes are to make protection truly effective.

Access to refugee-status determination

Tanzania is party to both the UN and African Refugee Conventions. And according to UNHCR, refugees from the DRC are still officially eligible for *prima facie* refugee status. But in practice, Tanzanian police patrolling Lake Tanganyika will sometimes demand a bribe or immediately turn away refugees attempting to enter Tanzanian territory. In 2003, UNHCR recorded 29 cases of actual refoulement on the lake.[20] When Congolese refugees do arrive on shore, they are directed to a reception centre outside Kigoma town, to be screened by immigration officials and the police.[21] The UNHCR has no oversight role in this process, and there are no records indicating the numbers of, or reasons for, any rejections.

Freedom of movement

Article 26 of the 1951 Refugee Convention provides that lawful refugees have the right to choose their place of residence and move freely within the host country. For refugees accommodated in camps for protracted periods, freedom of movement is a necessity denied. However, Tanzania maintains a policy of restricting refugee movement to an area within 4 km of a camp's outer perimeter. To leave Lugufu I or II, a refugee must obtain a permit from the Ministry of Home Affairs. Many refugees complain that the process takes too long, and that their requests are often denied. The penalty for unauthorised movements is six months' imprisonment, a fine of Tsh 50,000 (approximately $50), or both.[22] A 35-year-old primary-school teacher told us: *'If you want to move, you have to escape. If you are caught, you have a problem. Sometimes you have to chop wood, dig toilets, or cut trees for the police. Or they can ask for a bribe. If you can't pay, you'll be brought to the prison in town. There are cases of people staying there for even two years without their case being heard.'*

Nevertheless, there is a steady flow of refugees who leave the camps illegally, mainly to travel to Kigoma, where they can communicate with their relatives in the Congo, obtain medicine, or trade goods to supplement their sometimes inadequate or inappropriate assistance.

Assistance and access to employment

Congolese refugees residing in camps are given assistance to ensure, in the words of one donor, *'the bare minimum for survival'*. In general, the care and maintenance programmes provided meet international humanitarian standards. However, food rations are one persistent exception. According to the humanitarian SPHERE Standards, which set out the minimum requirements necessary to achieve 'life with dignity', the average nutritional requirement is 2100 kilocalories per person per day.[23] Refugees in the Lugufu camps receive 1842 kilocalories per day, provided through a subsistence ration of pulses, cereals, salt, oil, and corn–soya blend. In the past, refugees supplemented their diets by earning money from agricultural and casual labour for local Tanzanians, as well as trade in community markets. These opportunities have diminished considerably during the past several years. The government of Tanzania, citing security concerns, has chosen to vigorously enforce its policies restricting refugee movement outside the camps. This makes it difficult for refugees to take advantage of the sources of food and income that they previously enjoyed, which required travel outside the 4-km radius. In some of the Burundian camps, even the mixed markets where refugees traded foodstuffs with local communities have been closed. Furthermore, funding shortages led to supply problems for the World Food Programme (WFP) for a few months in 2003. During that time, rations fell as low as 1260 kilocalories per person per day. A WFP study published in July 2004 found that these developments have caused more people to reduce the size and numbers of meals, sell household assets, steal, engage in sex work, and even repatriate in order to cope.[24]

Access to durable solutions

The Tanzanian government espouses a policy of repatriation for all refugees. The current focus on repatriating the Burundian refugee population from Tanzania has deflected direct pressure from the Congolese, but most Congolese remain in limbo, without a durable solution in sight. Returning home is not an option for most, and integration into Tanzanian society is ruled out – as explained above. The third durable solution of resettlement has so far been open to only a tiny fraction of the refugees: only 495 refugees were resettled to third countries in 2003.[25]

Vulnerable groups

What constitutes 'effective protection' for one refugee is inadequate for another. In particular, women and ethnic minorities have more difficulty obtaining security and assistance than other refugees. There is only one UNHCR field staff person dedicated to protection in Lugufu I and II, in addition to two Kigoma-based protection officers who visit twice a week. They report that people most at risk fall into three categories: Banyamulenge, or Congolese Tutsis, who allege that they are harassed by the majority Bembe refugees at water points, in the nearby forests, and in other areas; people in mixed marriages of any kind; and people who are associated with the various warring factions in the Congo and fear revenge attacks by enemies in the camp.[26] Most new arrivals, in fact, assert that they are Banyamulenge or that they assisted the Rwandan-backed RCD during fighting in the DRC. These people are difficult to integrate into Lugufu. Indeed, the majority Bembe refugee population is openly hostile to the prospect of Banyamulenge arrivals, despite the fact that a number have lived quietly in the camp for years. As a 28-year-old man from Uvira explained, *'Before the war, we shared our lives with the Rwandans and attended the same schools. Now we are afraid to be with these people.'* Most refugees with Tutsi-like features are transferred directly to Mkugwa camp, with other at-risk groups.

Women and girls

Women and girls face unique problems of protection. The officer responsible for cases of gender-based violence in Lugufu I and II cites conflict, culture, and close living quarters in the camp as the prime causes. Domestic violence is most common, often affecting women with polygamous husbands, and survivors of sexual violence. Women who were raped during flight are frequently harassed, even disowned, by their ashamed families once they reach the relative security of the camp. Another widespread problem is forced marriage, particularly for recent widows, who face pressure from their in-laws to remarry within the family. Finally, rape is reported in the camps, particularly when the victim is a minor. From January through August 2004, there were 11 reported cases of rape, all perpetrated by other refugees, in Lugufu I and II.[27] These numbers represent only a fraction of actual incidents. Married women, who would face stigma and scepticism from the community should they lodge a complaint, are unlikely to acknowledge their assault. Judicial redress is not easy to achieve. In August 2004, only one case of rape involving a refugee survivor from Lugufu was being adjudicated in Kigoma courts.

What it means to live with dignity

The same factors driving some refugees to repatriate are spurring others to eke out marginal existences in towns like Kigoma. In order to gain the dignity of self-sufficiency and freedom, they work as small-scale traders, hairdressers, or casual labourers, loading bags of WFP food from the docks. Authorities estimate that there are about 10,000 unregistered Congolese in the Kigoma region, including fishermen who live in villages along the lake. But no matter how long they stay, most find it difficult to gain official status. One 66-year-old man, who fled from Uvira in 1962 and now lives in Mayobozi, told us, *'My life is a series of harassments. Two or three times a month the police will come and question me, and put me in prison until my wife bails me out. It's very hard – I try to fish, but I'm too old. The three hectares of land I bought is no longer fertile. Meanwhile, they [the police] can ask for Ts 10,000 ($10) or even Tsh 30,000. Becoming naturalised is difficult: you need a permit and you need to pay even more.'*

People interviewed in the outskirts of Kigoma pay regular bribes to the immigration officers and police. Despite daily threats of refoulement, these refugees preferred town life to the form of protection available in a contained camp. Dignity for them meant supporting themselves, communicating freely with their families in the Congo, and having a more varied and balanced diet. A 33-year-old Congolese woman living in Kigoma with her husband and four children told us: *'We left the camp six months ago, because the food wasn't sufficient. We walked for four days to Kigoma and at first stayed with a pastor in a church until he found us a house. We feel a bit more free here, but life is discouraging. There's no secondary school, and we have to hide with our neighbours every time immigration [officials] comes. If you don't have any money, they'll repatriate you. But still we get along by ourselves and do not have to wait for handouts.'*

Tool boxes and action plans

To strengthen protection in the regions, the Commission's June 2004 Communication proposed 'EU Regional Protection Programmes': a 'tool box' of actions and projects on asylum and migration to be initiated with regard to a specific region/country, and to be 'drawn up in partnership with the countries concerned'. These would also be formulated in conjunction with the Regional and Country Strategy Papers (R/CSPs), drawn up by the Commission's Development and External Relations Directorates, and as such would form part of the EU's overall strategy concerning the region or country in question: 'an integrated and comprehensive EU approach to asylum and migration'. The Hague Programme, agreed in November 2004, supports the June 2004 Communication and identifies RPPs as a core element of the EU's partnerships with countries and regions of origin.

The Commission plans to prepare a pilot Regional Protection Programme, for a protracted refugee situation to be identified in co-operation with the Council of the EU and with UNHCR. The Communication emphasises that these programmes would need to be both flexible and situation-specific and drawn up after an in-depth analysis of the refugee situation in the given region, to include a gaps analysis of the protection situation.[28] It hopes to finalise a plan of action by mid-2005, leading to a fully fledged Regional Protection Programme by December 2005.

Field-based knowledge, experience, and competence must be employed to ensure that different EU initiatives in a given region do not undermine each other.

The Programmes' 'tool boxes' would contain a range of activities, including:

- action to increase protection capacity;
- a registration scheme;
- an EU-wide resettlement scheme;
- assistance in improving the local infrastructure;
- assistance in local integration (presented primarily as a way to reduce secondary movements);
- co-operation on legal migration;
- action on migration management;
- and support for return, to be aimed at nationals of the country in question, as well as persons for whom that country 'has been or could have been a country of first asylum, if this country offers effective protection'.

The Commission has already funded some specific UNHCR projects to strengthen protection in regions of origin. These include a project supported by the Netherlands, Denmark, and the UK, which seeks to strengthen the protection capacity of four African countries: Kenya, Tanzania, Benin, and Burkina Faso. The project, which began in August 2004, is being implemented by UNHCR. It seeks first to identify existing protection gaps in these countries, then to propose measures to address these gaps, and then to implement them, once support has been secured.[29]

In the longer term, if the EU is serious about improving the conditions for refugees in a given region, policy makers and implementers must be well informed about conditions in that region, *at all stages of project development, implementation, and evaluation.* The proposed initiatives could have a significant, positive impact, but only if EU action is informed by a full understanding of the realities of the specific refugee situations in which they are intervening. Field-based knowledge, experience, and competence must be employed to ensure that different EU initiatives in a given region do not serve to undermine each other.

The Commission intends that host communities in regions of origin should be 'actively involved' in EU action to improve local infrastructure.[30] As with resettlement, an EU body based in the relevant region could oversee implementation and monitor the impact of EU activities as part of a regular review process. It could also serve as an effective forum for consultation with local communities; without a localised forum, effective dialogue between host/refugee communities and policy makers based in the EU could become impossible. In this respect, there are lessons to be learned from the experiences of the High Level Working Group, whose 'Action Plans' were drawn up without such consultation, as discussed in Chapter 7. Similar criticisms have been made of the two International Conferences on Refugees in Africa (ICARA), organised in the early 1980s, which sought to assist the local integration of refugees in Africa yet failed to find common ground between Western and African governments and failed to consult with refugees themselves.[31]

Unanswered questions, mixed motivations

As we have seen in previous chapters, doubts exist about the true motivations at the heart of proposals for orderly entry. Like resettlement, 'regional protection programmes' have the potential to make a genuinely positive impact. They could improve the quality of protection accorded to individual refugees, and also represent concrete acts of responsibility sharing, perhaps encouraging other states to act likewise. However, with pilot projects at such an early stage, Regional Protection proposals raise many unanswered questions. It is hard to see how the EU might begin to achieve its ambitious agenda of providing effective protection in regions where such protection has been denied to millions for decades.

The effective implementation of a regional protection programme would demand a high and sustained level of financial and human resources.

In particular, the issues of finance and responsibility for projects are not clearly defined. The effective implementation of a regional protection programme would demand a high and sustained level of financial and human resources. However, it remains unclear whether these would come from the Justice and Home Affairs budget or from existing development and external relations programming. This would make a big difference to the direction of the programmes. With a development/external relations remit, activities would seek to enhance conditions in the regions as an end in itself; whereas, with a JHA remit, enhancing protection could be seen as instrumental to migration management. If it is to be a joint remit, then co-ordination is crucial. Past experience has highlighted the practical difficulties of implementing cross-departmental action plans (see Chapter 7).

Policy papers from the UK government,[32] the European Commission,[33] and the Dutch government [34] assume a 'migration management' impact (i.e. that protection in the regions will lead to fewer asylum speakers arriving 'spontaneously' in the EU). This assumption is questionable. In theory, if a situation can be reached where standards of protection in a region of origin can be significantly improved through comprehensive and targeted action, this may indeed reduce the need for some persons in that region to move onwards and seek better protection elsewhere. However, this would require long-term and significant commitment, and EU member states should not expect to see any significant results in the short to medium term.

The European Commission itself accepts that there is 'a long way to go before most of the current refugee hosting countries in the regions of origin could be considered to meet such a standard where they are able and willing to offer effective protection', and indeed that 'some countries may take decades before they can reach the institutional and infrastructural standards required'.[35] In this context, therefore, it is imperative that EU policy makers do not view Regional Protection Programmes as means to achieve short-term migration-management goals.

The migration-management agenda also raises the prospect of further geo-politicisation of refugee assistance. An overview of global spending on aid reveals a clear bias towards responding to crises that are publicised in the international media, while others remain forgotten. Through ECHO, EU has probably done more than any other donor to give assistance according to needs, after being criticised for favouring crises such as those in the former Yugoslavia over those farther afield.[36] The migration-management agenda threatens to challenge this, and those countries from which refugees do not travel to the EU may be forgotten. Certain regions or groups of refugees could be targeted on the basis of possible secondary movement to the EU, rather than on the basis of vulnerability and protection needs. For example, Dutch ministries have commented that 'the more asylum seekers come from a particular region, the greater is the Netherlands' interest in consolidating protection there'.[37]

The Communication also suggests that the Programmes could add to the EU's bargaining power when negotiating partnership agreements with third countries on asylum and immigration matters: the potential benefits of an RPP for the third country concerned could be used as an incentive to encourage that country to, for example, conclude readmission agreements with the EU.

Recent developments: processing centres back on the agenda?

During the Dutch Presidency of the EU, certain events (in particular the *Cap Anamur* incident – see Chapter 4) led some EU member states to re-open the debate on external processing centres, begun by the UK's 'New Vision' proposals. Otto Schilly, the interior minister for Germany (initially one of the member states most strongly opposed to the original 'New Vision' plan), has reopened the debate with a call for 'EU asylum centres' to be created in North Africa, staffed by officials from member states, with the aim of deciding 'who is allowed to enter the continent'.[38] Although the precise details of the proposal remain vague, it appears that Germany favours setting up such a centre in Tunisia. Italy responded enthusiastically to the idea and appears to favour creating a processing camp in Libya.[39]

The 2004 Hague Programme calls for a study to examine the 'merits, appropriateness and feasibility of joint processing of asylum applications *outside* EU territory'.[40] This re-emergence of the UK's proposal for Transit Processing Centres on the official EU agenda shows the strength of political will in favour of an idea that had been widely discredited only the year before.[41]

With the current emphasis on migration management, and the re-emergence of the plan for TPCs, there is the disturbing possibility that EU member states may in the future use 'protection in the region' initiatives, and a restrictive interpretation of 'effective protection', to justify the return of persons in need of protection from the EU to their region of origin. Large-scale returns to a region where the EU is simultaneously attempting to increase protection capacity may serve to undermine those very efforts. This would negate the potential use of such initiatives to strengthen the international protection regime, and undermine the claim that such initiatives will represent genuine sharing of responsibility by the EU.

Recommendations

Principles

- Transit processing camps should not be established, because they would amount to shifting the burden of caring for Europe's refugees on to poor countries which could not guarantee their safety.
- EU efforts to increase protection capacity in regions of origin could make a positive contribution to international refugee protection and could be concrete acts of responsibility sharing.
- However, Regional Protection Programmes (RPPs) must not be used as bargaining chips by the EU to encourage third countries to co-operate in managing migration, or to accept returns, particularly of third-country nationals. Member states' support for RPPs should not be contingent on short-term migration-management goals which are unlikely to be met.
- Host countries of refugee populations must undertake to guarantee the realisation of refugees' full rights within their available resources. Refugees should not be used as scapegoats for political ends, nor unnecessarily warehoused in refugee camps and so denied the opportunity of local integration.

Application

- RPPs should comprise well-resourced, long-term initiatives which are targeted according to an assessment of real needs for protection in the regions and countries in question, based on a full and inclusive interpretation of effective protection.
- At this stage, much greater clarity is required about the aims, contents, and resourcing of RPPs. Their development and future implementation should be based on transparent dialogue with stakeholders in the region (refugee communities, UNHCR, NGOs, and governments), as well as policy coherence with existing EU development and humanitarian activities in the regions/countries.
- Governments in the region must ensure that refugee protection and the welfare of the host communities are paramount in this dialogue with the EU, above political or financial gains.

Countries of origin: the root causes of refugee flows 7

COUNTRIES FOR WHICH ACTION PLANS WERE DRAWN UP BY THE EU HIGH LEVEL WORKING GROUP ON ASYLUM AND MIGRATION IN 2000

Afghanistan/Pakistan • Albania
Morocco • Somalia • Sri Lanka • Iraq

Mukulya IDP camp, Beni, Democratic Republic of Congo, February 2004
© Jane Beesley / Oxfam GB

7
Countries of origin: the root causes of refugee flows

> *The European Union needs a comprehensive approach to migration, addressing political, human rights and development issues in countries and regions of origin and transit. This requires combating poverty, improving living conditions and job opportunities, preventing conflicts and consolidating democratic states and ensuring respect for human rights, in particular rights of minorities, women and children.*
> European Council, Tampere, October 1999 [1]
>
> *Goal 1,12: States to give greater priority to dealing with root causes, including armed conflict, and to ensure relevant intergovernmental agendas reflect this priority.*
>
> *States to use appropriate means at their disposal, in the context of their foreign, security, trade, development and investment policies, to influence developments in refugee-producing countries in the direction of greater respect for human rights, democratic values and good governance.*
> UNHCR Agenda for Protection [2]

The impact of EU external policy actions

Throughout the debate on a comprehensive and global approach to immigration and asylum there has been a growing awareness of the need to address 'root causes' – the reasons why people flee their homes in the first place – as well as dealing with them after they have fled. Virtually all EU external actions have some direct or indirect bearing on the causes of forced and economic migration. More than any other aspect of the 'internationalised agenda', 'root causes' raise difficult questions of policy coherence or co-ordination between the home affairs, development, and external relations divisions.

The first section of this chapter will consider some aspects of EU policies which may affect refugee flows. While a detailed examination of each of these issues is beyond the scope of the present study, this chapter will focus on human rights, conflict prevention, humanitarian assistance, development, and arms-trade policy. The second section will examine the general approach of EU policy makers to addressing root causes, and also the need for 'joined-up' EU policy making as a means to achieve these goals.

The reasons why people flee their homes in the first place are diverse and complex. At a basic level, the Convention definition tells us that a refugee is someone fleeing persecution, i.e. human-rights violations. People can also be forced to flee their homes by widespread conflict and violence. But the causes of human-rights abuses, conflict, and violence are embedded in deep-rooted social, economic, and political conditions.

How is external EU policy made?

The main aims of the EU's Common Foreign and Security Policy (CFSP) include: 'to preserve peace and strengthen international security, in accordance with the principles of the United Nations Charter [..]', 'to promote international co-operation', and 'to develop and consolidate democracy and the rule of law, and respect for human rights and fundamental freedoms'.[3]

The European Council defines general principles and guidelines for CFSP, and adopts common strategies. In this way CFSP is an inter-governmental area of EU activity; while they may seek co-ordinated action, individual member states retain primary control over such policies. A relatively new part of the CFSP is the European Security and Defence Policy (ESDP), which covers all matters relating to EU security.

While the role of the European Commission in CFSP is fairly restricted, in contrast the Commission is solely responsible for other areas of external EU activity, such as trade, humanitarian response, and development assistance. Overall, the Council and the Commission work jointly to ensure consistency of EU external activities as a whole, in the context of its policies on external relations, security, economic matters, and development.

Human rights

Human-rights violations and refugee movements

A refugee is someone who has a 'well-founded' fear of suffering persecution if returned to his or her country of origin.[4] While there is no single, precise definition of 'persecution' within international law, it is generally accepted that persecution is the serious or sustained violation of fundamental human rights. Recognising someone as a 'refugee' is primarily a way for states to protect individuals from suffering human-rights violations. Promoting respect for human-rights principles, and acting to reduce the frequency and gravity of human-rights abuses in refugees' countries of origin, is central to any initiative to address the 'root causes' of forced migration.

How does the EU promote human rights abroad?

Respect for human rights is fundamental to the legal order of the European Union. The Treaty of Amsterdam reaffirmed that the EU is 'founded on the principles of liberty, democracy, respect for human rights and fundamental freedoms, and the rule of law'.[5] This was underlined with the proclamation, in 2000, of the Charter of Fundamental Rights of the European Union. At present, the Charter is not legally binding on member states. Under the EU Constitutional Treaty, however, the Union as a whole would accede to the Charter, which would then become binding on members and could be used to challenge the validity of subsequent Community legislation. Importantly, the European Council has affirmed that this would place the Union under a legal obligation to act in line with the Charter, in all areas of EU activity.[6]

As discussed, one of the explicit objectives of the EU's external action is the development and consolidation of democracy and the rule of law, and respect for human rights. The EU has a number of instruments to achieve these objectives, including diplomatic representations, financial support to civil-society bodies, and human-rights clauses in trade and co-operation agreements, which allow the EU to suspend the agreement if the third country fails to uphold standards of human rights.

The European Commission has asserted that the EU is well placed to promote human rights and democratisation effectively, but has also acknowledged that this aspiration requires greater policy coherence.[7] As with asylum and migration, human rights and democratisation are relevant to many different EU policy areas.

Considerable effort is required to ensure that one type of EU policy (for example security-related initiatives) does not undermine projects designed to promote respect for, and observance of, international human-rights principles. EU immigration-control policies, in particular, are sometimes implemented in a way which contradicts statements and actions made elsewhere by the EU in support of human-rights principles (see Box 11, below).

Conflict management

How does conflict influence refugee flows?

While the causal relationships involved are complex, it is widely accepted that violent conflict increases the likelihood, and the extent, of forced migration from a given country.[8] Violent conflict can create situations where the existing state apparatus breaks down, where overall state capacity is reduced, and state funds are diverted to the security sector. In such a situation, state authorities often become unwilling or unable to provide adequate protection for their own population.

Violent conflict can lead to widespread human-rights violations and insecurity, forcing many people to flee their homes. One 30-year-old woman who recently arrived in Tanzania from the east of the Democratic Republic of Congo (DRC) described how conflict continues to terrorise civilians, taking the form of individual persecution which forces them to flee their homes:

> *One night in June, I heard gunshots, and in the morning we found that 15 Tutsi neighbours had been killed, and we buried them. Not long afterwards, a car full of men approached me and asked about the mass grave. I showed them where it was. A few days later, my neighbour found me at the market and told me my house was burning, and that people planned to kill me because I support the Banyamulenge. I ran to the church pastor with my baby, but I had to leave my three other children, and my husband, behind. He arranged for my transport to Kigoma. I have no home. My parents are dead. I don't know where my family is. I had never heard the term 'Banyamulenge' until the war started. Now I can never think about going back to the Congo.*

The devastating impact of violent conflict may be clear, but it is often far from clear how the international community can best address this root cause of forced migration. Attempting to limit, or even prevent, the outbreak of violent conflict may involve tackling sensitive issues related to state sovereignty, and for this reason it will continue to pose a challenge to the international community.[9]

Even the most determined of diplomatic efforts can fail when the parties to a conflict are locked in violence; peace-keeping measures or, exceptionally, peace enforcement may be needed. The Rwandan genocide has shown that the difference between international action and inaction can be measured in the lives of thousands, and the forced displacement of many more.[10]

What does the EU do to prevent conflict?

The UN Security Council (UNSC) bears primary responsibility for maintaining international peace and security. Two of the five permanent members of the UN Security Council, the UK and France, are EU member states. The Security Council is charged with responding to threats to peace, breaches of peace, or acts of aggression. It has a range of measures at its disposal for this purpose, ranging from political measures and sanctions to the use of force where the situation requires.[11] On numerous occasions, the UNSC has invoked human-rights violations as a justification for action under Chapter VII of its Charter. In late 2003, the UN Secretary General established a 'High Level Panel on Threats, Challenges and Change', to ensure that the UN is capable of fulfilling its primary aim: the prevention and removal of threats to the peace.[12]

While conflict prevention is not an explicit goal of the EU's foreign and security policy,[13] there are numerous documents in which the Union commits itself to be active in this area.[14] Many different types of EU activity, using both civilian and military means, aim to prevent conflict and manage crises. They range from diplomatic engagements where EU Special Representatives have been sent to 'hotspots' (such as the Middle East, and the Great Lakes region), and EU Conflict Prevention Assessment missions (such as those sent to Sri Lanka, Indonesia, and Nepal in 2002),[15] to sending EU civilian or military personnel to assist in peace keeping, crisis management, and policing. EU missions include Operation Artemis in the DRC and 'Proxima', the EU Police Mission in Macedonia. An explicit goal of Proxima is to support 'the operational transition towards, and the creation of a border police, as a part of the wider EU effort to promote integrated border management'.[16]

The Rwandan genocide has shown that the difference between international action and inaction can be measured in the lives of thousands, and the forced displacement of many more.

In addition, the Council has recently developed a new Rapid Reaction Mechanism, designed for urgent interventions in crises. RRM funds can be used to restore the rule of law and promote democracy and human rights, as well as for peace-building and mediation initiatives, demobilisation and reintegration of combatants, and reconstruction activities.[17] The RRM was seen by some EU policy makers as a possible mechanism for evacuating large numbers of asylum seekers (from Turkey, for example) to the EU in the event of the predicted mass exodus from Iraq in mid-2003.

Civil-society organisations can play a range of crucial roles in advancing peace; without the involvement of civil society, states may struggle to prevent or resolve violent conflict. The EU has attempted to encourage civil-society participation in conflict-prevention initiatives (for example, through the frameworks of the Cotonou Agreement between the EU and the African, Caribbean, and Pacific (ACP) group of states, and, at least on paper, in the Stability Pact for South-Eastern Europe). However, attempts by EU policy makers to involve civil society in important political dialogue may also be informal and *ad hoc*.[18]

An important innovation of the Cotonou Agreement (which provides for co-operation in terms of politics, trade, and development) was the emphasis that it placed on the need for links with civil society in the ACP countries. In implementing the Cotonou Agreement, however, EU policy makers have found it difficult to find effective interlocutors, because the strength of civil society in ACP regions varies widely from country to country; so the EU has sought to build capacity where it is lacking. An internationalised EU asylum agenda will necessitate greater consultation and information sharing between EU policy makers and field-based actors. It is important that the channels for consultation established in the context of the Cotonou Agreement are fully utilised; where such channels are lacking, policy makers must learn from the lessons of Cotonou in seeking to develop effective interlocutors.

Development co-operation

How does development influence refugee flows?

As underlying factors influencing the movements of asylum seekers to Europe, indicators of conflict have been found to be far more significant than indicators of development. But the links between conflict, under-development, and forced migration are real and complex. For example, it is often true that conflict can itself undermine on-going development efforts in a given country, or indeed that conflict may itself be 'an expression of underdevelopment or a failed development strategy'.[19]

Development co-operation is often essential in the search for durable solutions to refugee problems.

Development co-operation is often essential in the search for durable solutions to refugee problems. In Tanzania, development assistance has also been directed to assist the local communities that host refugees, increasing their capacity to absorb them, and reducing the possibility of tensions between the refugee and local populations.

Targeted development co-operation can also reduce the chances of subsequent forced displacement and help to ensure that refugee repatriation is sustainable. However, it is important to distinguish between measures to create conditions for return, and measures to address the root causes of forced migration. Providing durable solutions, such as enabling sustainable and voluntary repatriation, is a crucial, yet distinct, goal. However, it is a reactive measure; it is not a proactive measure which addresses why people flee their homes in the first place. Addressing the root causes of forced migration means addressing human-rights violations and violent conflicts *in countries of origin*, not limiting onward movement from countries in the region or countries of transit. The EU's focus on countries in the region and countries of transit has shifted attention away from the need to address root causes.

How have concerns about asylum and migration influenced EU action on development?

EU actions have repeatedly linked development co-operation with migration/asylum issues.[20] The Seville European Council marked an important stage in the developing relationship between EU development policy and its policy on asylum and migration. As discussed in Chapter 4, in Seville the member states proposed making development assistance to third countries contingent on their co-operation in fighting illegal immigration to the EU. Instead of aiming to reduce levels of forced migration through long-term, targeted development co-operation, therefore, the approach proposed at Seville could see levels of development assistance being reduced in response to ongoing emigration or onward migration. Reduced

> **Box 9 Risks for returnees to the Democratic Republic of Congo**
>
> Any future migration-management co-operation between the EU and the DRC must reflect the protection threats that confront asylum seekers upon their return to the DRC. Congolese NGOs such as *La Voix des Sans Voix* have documented numerous cases of arbitrary detention and ill treatment by the security forces of people who sought asylum abroad. Furthermore, people from the east may be stranded in Kinshasa, where they face discrimination, harassment, and indefinite separation from their families.
>
> '*When I was sent back to Kinshasa, soldiers were waiting for me. Fortunately a stranger from a human-rights group met my plane and took me out of the airport. I know someone who was asked to pay $300 in return for his freedom. Now I live with a friend whom I met at the detention centre in England. I have no money, and no family. There is no one to help me. My Lingala is bad, so they [the security forces] think I'm a spy from Rwanda. How can I return home?*' – Congolese man from Bukavu, recently removed from the UK

levels of development assistance to certain countries could make conflict-prevention efforts less effective, which in turn could *increase* the likelihood of forced migration from these countries.

This approach was also noticeable in the negotiation of the EU agreements on trade and aid with 70 ACP countries. Towards the end of the negotiations leading to the Lomé IV Convention in early 2000, the EU insisted, in spite of strong opposition by ACP countries, on the insertion of a clause on the readmission and repatriation of illegal migrants. The resulting Cotonou Agreement, which will run until 2020, strengthens the position of the EU on readmission agreements.[21] It is a cause for concern that the relevant clause of the Cotonou Agreement commits ACP states to readmit their nationals at the request of EU member states 'and without further formalities'. Such 'formalities' often provide crucial safety nets to protect the rights of those in need of international protection.

Humanitarian assistance

How does the EU provide humanitarian assistance?

Humanitarian assistance comprises a range of activities to mitigate the consequences of conflicts and natural disasters.[22] The provision of humanitarian assistance is intended less to prevent the root causes of forced migration than to *minimise their impact* on local populations. As with development co-operation, humanitarian assistance can not only play a crucial role in reducing the need for people to flee from their homes, but can help to create a situation where safe and sustainable return becomes possible.

The EC's relief operations are handled by ECHO, its humanitarian aid office. ECHO co-ordinates the response to humanitarian emergencies, while relying on humanitarian partners – including NGOs, some UN agencies, and the ICRC – to implement a range of emergency programme activities. ECHO supports UNCHR to implement its mandate of protecting refugees by funding UNHCR's protection, security, and registration operations. The EC's humanitarian assistance has three main tools: emergency aid, food aid, and aid for persons who have been displaced by conflict (including both refugees and IDPs).

By their nature, disaster relief and emergency assistance might appear to be short-term operations only. However, in emergencies it is essential that, when humanitarian aid is withdrawn, the population involved can cope with the situation, and that a longer-term development / reconstruction strategy is in place. The cyclical nature of many humanitarian crises may mean that, even when the immediate emergency is over, populations are still left with poor infrastructure and inadequate protection. This insecurity, in turn, often forces people to (again) flee their homes. Significantly, ECHO emphasises the needs, not only of refugees and IDPs, but also of returnees – as in Afghanistan and Sri Lanka.[23]

ECHO's commitment to provide assistance solely on the basis of humanitarian needs, and not according to political considerations, is important. So is the fact that, in identifying high-need crises, it combines 'a bottom–up view (field level) [...] with a top–down approach to identify high-need humanitarian crises that receive low media and donor attention'.[24] This approach should also be applied to the 'internationalised asylum agenda': policy making in the field of asylum must respond to need and incorporate the knowledge and experience of field-based actors (the 'bottom–up view').

Box 10 Root causes of conflict and forced displacement in the DRC

'Innocent people are rotting in jail, splitting firewood for warders' wives without trial, while the real killers are drinking beer every evening with those who should arrest them.'

The situation in the Democratic Republic of Congo illustrates the difficulty of addressing the root causes of a conflict which has directly involved some six countries during the past eight years. These causes are too complex to describe in any detail here; but, in simplified form, some of the (inter-related) factors include the following:

- *The colonial legacy of corrupt governance, impunity, and exploitation of divisions between groups.*[25] From the early days of Belgian rule, through the Mobutu regime and beyond, the Congo has been grossly mismanaged by autocrats who consolidated personal control over state resources, manipulated ethnic identities, and sanctioned mass violations of human rights. According to one observer, *'Innocent people [throughout the region] are rotting in jail, splitting firewood for warders' wives without trial, while the real killers are drinking beer every evening with those who should arrest them.'*[26]

- *The legacy of the Cold War.* Like most developing countries that gained independence in Latin America and Africa after the Second World War, the DRC was a proxy battleground for the Cold War. The conflict between the Western and Eastern blocs killed the first democratically elected head of state, encouraged a secessionist war, and set up the puppet regime of Mobutu Sese Seko. For his loyalty to the West, Mobutu received unwavering support, despite his dictatorial and undemocratic practices; this support was to last until the collapse of the Eastern bloc. The seeds of conflict eventually grew on very fertile ground: a mis-governed country, shocking levels of poverty in a land of plenty, and neglected provinces where the state was absent.

- *Demographic pressures in Rwanda and Burundi*, countries which have too little land to accommodate their growing populations. Both countries, at various points, have aggressively exported extra labour to the eastern parts of DRC.

- *Exploitation of the DRC's coltan, diamonds, copper, cobalt, and gold.* This is both a root cause and an immediate cause of conflict. The governments of DRC, Uganda, Rwanda, and other countries fund their armies through the sale of mining and forestry concessions, the production of and trade in commodities, and the collection of customs and taxes in territories under their control. The vast profits to be gained from this exploitation create little incentive for the various groups to put an end to fighting.

- *Hutu–Tutsi tensions*.[27] Belgian policies encouraging migration of Rwandans into the Kivus after World War I led to tensions with indigenous residents, whose land was sold to the settlers by local chiefs. Since Laurent Kabila's seizure of power in 1996, the Banyamulenge have suffered discrimination, harassment, and worse because of their identification with Rwandan interlopers. As long as conflict continues, all factions will use ethnic factors to justify their military actions.

EU action in DRC

Considering the current instability, most assistance to the DRC is focused on humanitarian relief, security-sector reform, and initiatives to reduce conflict. The disarmament, demobilisation, and reintegration (DDR) processes for foreign and national forces are key to establishing peace in the short term. The national disarmament programme for Ituri district, with a budget of $10.5 million (approximately €8,000,000), began in September 2004.

However, the process is moving slowly, and many observers express concern that reintegration assistance is inadequate to provide viable alternatives to the ex-combatants, particularly those above school age who have no income-generating skills. Of the 330,000 Congolese in the national army waiting to be demobilised, only around 100,000 would be absorbed by the new integrated army.[28] That leaves more than two-thirds of the forces in need of alternative opportunities. There are also an estimated 8000–12,000 foreign soldiers from the Forces Démocratiques de Libération du Rwanda (FDLR) still at large in South Kivu.[29] Several factions have not agreed to disarm at all, and others fund their military operations by selling concessions, trading in commodities, and collecting taxes in territories that they control. The profits to be gained from mineral exploitation mean there is little incentive for the various groups to end the conflict.

Like other major donors in the DRC, the EU is keen to establish sufficient security for a successful national election in 2005. In addition to its financial support to DDR through the World Bank's Multi-Country Demobilization and Reintegration Program, the main activities with a direct impact on civilian protection include the following:

- *Conflict de-escalation*. As a means of controlling fighting in Ituri district in mid-2003, the EU launched Operation Artemis with 1400 troops under French command. Artemis was considered successful in achieving its limited objectives: it was able to stabilise the situation around Bunia city in time for MONUC reinforcements to be deployed. It also demonstrated the EU's capacity to link various instruments at its disposal to address conflict in third countries. For example, the Rapid Reaction Mechanism fast-tracked the disbursement of nearly one million euro after Operation Artemis, to support urgent reforms of the justice sector in Bunia.

- *Development assistance*. The EU and its member states, particularly Belgium, France, and the UK, have shown strong support for the transitional national government that was agreed to in Pretoria in December 2002. The current EU Country Strategy Paper (CSP) for the DRC (committing €205,000,000 to cover the period 2003–2007) was signed in September 2003, during a joint ECHO–DEV–AIDCO–Delegation mission to the country.[30] It is the first official development funding since aid was unilaterally suspended by the EU and other donors in 1991. In 1995, under a humanitarian cover, the EU resumed support for sectors such as roads and health. As in other ACP countries, the European Development Fund (EDF) is the main instrument for EU development assistance.

The CSP proposes three categories of high-priority action: (1) anti-poverty measures focused on the health sector; (2) institutional support for the democratic transitional process leading to elections; and (3) macro-economic support.[31] Other priority sectors include good governance and rule of law. The mid-term review of the CSP in 2004 resulted in increased funds for infrastructure, but no other major changes.[32]

- *Humanitarian aid*. Humanitarian aid, especially in the east, is explicitly framed as a form of conflict reduction.[33] ECHO's key objectives in the DRC are to contain major epidemics, increase access for war-affected populations to basic health care, reduce acute malnutrition, and provide emergency relief for newly displaced families and returnees.[34] Geographically, ECHO focuses on the Greater Kivu and Ituri areas and recently accessible areas along the former front lines (Equateur, Kasai, and Katanga provinces). ECHO also provides funding to certain international agencies, such as the ICRC and UNOCHA, to support their protection and co-ordination activities. It functions in a 'humanitarian plus' capacity, channelling approximately 50 per cent of its funds into the existing health-care system.[35] In 2004, ECHO spent approximately €45,000,000 on projects in the DRC.[36]

- *Security-sector reform*. In addition to funding the national disarmament programme, the EU recently launched a project to train 1008 officers for the Unit for Protection of Institutions (UPI), which will eventually take over from MONUC. The immediate priority for these police will be to ensure security before and during the elections.
- *Justice-sector reform*. With other donors, the EU recently concluded an audit to identify current needs in the justice sector. It also supports the Belgian NGO Réseau Citoyens Network (RCN Justice et Démocratie) to build the capacity and infrastructure of the justice system in Bunia. The initial phase of this project ended in June 2004. To complement domestic efforts such as the one in Bunia, the International Criminal Court (ICC) chose Ituri district as the site of its first official investigation.[37] The ICC will target the most serious war crimes and crimes against humanity, including summary executions, rape, and child recruitment. Observers hope that high-profile prosecutions of still-active armed elements in Ituri will deter future abuses.

Stopping the fighting before dealing with root causes

Given the imperative to contain current fighting, it is not surprising that long-term action to address root causes of displacement is somewhat overshadowed by immediate demands. While some of the actions to contain the fighting will have longer-term impacts, major long-term root causes such as the exploitation of Congo's natural resources have hardly been addressed by donors. One exception is the UK government's Department for International Development (DFID), which supports Global Witness's investigative research into the issue. Also, despite the clear regional dimension of the conflict, most regional initiatives remain at the political, not programmatic, level.[38] The EU's Special Envoy for the Great Lakes Region, for example, maintains dialogue with African States, the UN, and the Organisation of Africa Unity.

Arms-trade policies

How does the arms trade influence refugee flows?

Arms transfers may be crucial to support the legitimate security needs of a state. However, if arms transfers are not to undermine development and increase the likelihood of forced migration, the potential security benefits must be weighed against the long-term development needs of the country, and the human rights of its people.[39]

Often the funds that developing countries spend on arms and military equipment could instead be used to support on-going development projects. In some cases, imported arms have fuelled the brutal exploitation of resources in developing countries, with the result that natural resources which could have facilitated development have instead been used to fund conflict and repression. In this way, arms trading can increase the likelihood of forced migration, as seen in Angola, Sierra Leone, Liberia, and the Democratic Republic of Congo.[40]

Arms trading can also negatively affect development efforts in refugee-hosting countries. As well as fuelling insecurity, large-scale arms trading with countries hosting significant numbers of refugees can mean the diversion of funds from important development objectives.[41] This could limit the capacity of these countries to strengthen local infrastructure in a way which would be beneficial not only for local populations but also for refugees living in these countries. In this way, arms trading can have an indirect, yet significant, impact on the need for forced migrants to leave their country of first asylum and seek protection elsewhere.

Ignoring international responsibilities: facilitating human-rights violations

Arms transfers should be allowed only to countries with governments and accountable armed forces which are trained to uphold the standards of international human rights and humanitarian law. Arms transfers to countries where such standards are regularly flouted may mean that the arms are used to violate human rights and facilitate undemocratic rule. In particular, violence against women is notably widespread in heavily armed environments.[42]

There are many major arms suppliers in the EU, including three of the six largest arms suppliers in the world (UK, France, and Germany), some of which continue to undertake arms deals without regard for the long-term consequences. The UK government, for example, has allowed British companies to supply weapons to armed forces in the DRC that are responsible for mass abuses of human rights, and has continued supplying arms to Nepal in spite of severe civil unrest in that country. Successive French governments have provided military equipment to numerous francophone countries in Africa, often regardless of the human-rights records of some of them.[43]

The EU Code of Conduct on Arms Exports (CoC, agreed in June 1998) has led to greater transparency and accountability in EU arms exports. However, the code contains some serious weaknesses which are not yet being addressed by member states, leaving the EU out of step with progress in other regional forums, including the Organization for Security and Co-operation in Europe (OSCE) and the Nairobi Protocol. It also fails to reflect the requirement for states to authorise arms transfers in accordance with 'existing responsibilities under international law' set out in the UN Programme of Action on Small Arms and Light Weapons.[44]

There is much evidence that some EU member states continue to take advantage of ambiguous wording in the CoC, with the result that exports of arms to undemocratic and unstable countries have not ceased.[45] EU governments have largely failed to make an adequate assessment of the impact of these exports on poverty in recipient countries, where arms sales often divert funds from health and education programmes, and serve to endanger the security and human rights of the population.[46]

These failures to control arms exports mean that EU arms sales are not helping to reduce violent conflict in recipient countries. In this way, EU practices could serve to accentuate the root causes of forced migration. In view of this, governments need to agree an international Arms Trade Treaty, to control the arms trade in a way that will safeguard sustainable development and human rights.

Recommendations

Principles

- Policy coherence is necessary to ensure that the EU's external actions address rather than exacerbate forced migration, and that the home-affairs migration-management actions are not at odds with human rights, development, and humanitarian objectives.

Application

- In implementing aspects of the 'internationalised' asylum agenda, EU policy makers should take advantage of pre-existing channels of communication and forums which have been established in other areas of EU policy (in the context of the Cotonou Agreement, for example).

- EU asylum policy makers should draw on the experience of ECHO and seek to combine a bottom–up view with a top–down approach to ensure that projects are chosen and implemented according to the need for protection.

- Targeted development assistance can make an essential contribution to the design of durable solutions, supporting host communities and reducing displacement in the long term. Development assistance must not be made conditional on 'migration management' co-operation.

- EU policy makers should ensure that migration-management initiatives do not undermine or contradict EU action to promote human rights.

- EU member states must respect their international humanitarian and human-rights responsibilities if engaging in the supply of arms; must adequately assess the potential impact of their arms exports on volatile situations; and seek agreement on an international Arms Trade Treaty, to control arms in a way that will safeguard sustainable development and human rights.

Box 11 Selling arms to Libya – another example of policy incoherence?

Unregulated arms trading by the EU could compromise the rights of asylum seekers and refugees already living in third countries. A clear example is the recent decision by the EU to lift the embargo on the trading of arms or other military equipment to Libya. The embargo was originally adopted in 1986, in response to Libya's 'support for terrorism'.[47] In September 2003, the Italian Presidency of the EU proposed lifting it, to allow the supply of 'non lethal weapons and their platforms' to Libya, to enable the latter to better pursue the 'fight against illegal immigration'. In October the Council of the EU agreed to fully lift the embargo on arms sales to Libya.[48]

The Council stressed that any transfers to Libya will be subject to the Code of Conduct on Arms Exports, and pledged to 'follow closely the human rights situation in Libya'. However, Oxfam, believing that these safeguards are insufficient, is seriously concerned that military equipment sold to Libya by EU member states may be used in a way which violates the rights of refugees, asylum seekers, and other migrants in Libya.

The same Council Conclusions which confirmed the lifting of the embargo expressed 'immediate concern' regarding 'serious impediments to the right of free speech and association, credible reports of torture of suspects and miscarriages of justice and inhuman conditions of detention' in Libya. The decisive factor for member states, however, appears not to have been these grave human-rights concerns, but rather the consideration that 'co-operation with Libya on migrations is essential and urgent'.

While the Council emphasised that Libya 'should respect its international obligations', numerous reports show that asylum seekers in Libya remain subject to indefinite detention and forcible deportations.[49] Libya has not acceded to the 1951 Refugee Convention; and, while it has signed the 1969 OAU Refugee Convention, there are at present no domestic procedures for asylum seekers arriving in, or sent back to, Libya. UNHCR has no formal legal framework for operating in Libya, and is often denied access to asylum seekers who are returned there.[50]

For Libya to 'assist in the fight against illegal immigration', as the EU demands, may mean further restrictions of movement and detention of asylum seekers, and possible refoulement of persons in need of international protection. By sending military equipment to Libya for 'immigration control' purposes, the EU may well be facilitating these violations of human rights.

Coherence or co-operation? Joined-up EU policy

Although basic coherence between EU domestic and external policies on asylum has often been lacking, plans for co-operation on the root causes of refugee flows and immigration have featured on the EU agenda over the past ten years. However, these have been largely ineffective, due to a lack of investment and consultation with the countries in question. They have also been marred by a domination of home-affairs concerns (to prevent irregular migration to the EU), rather than development, humanitarian, or human-rights concerns (to tackle the poverty, persecution, conflict, and inequality that cause forced migration). As a result, in recent years the need to address 'root causes' has slipped off the EU agenda, despite frequent acknowledgment of its importance. From some positive and inclusive explorations of root causes by EU policy makers in the early 1990s, there has been a marked shift in debate away from the root causes of migration from countries of origin to the root causes of migration from countries of transit to the EU.

From Edinburgh to Seville

A 'root cause' approach to EU asylum and immigration policy has been on the agenda on and off for at least ten years. As early as December 1992, the European Council recognised 'the importance of analysing the causes of immigration pressure and analysing ways of removing the causes of migratory movements'. It called for increased co-ordination across the range of EU activities concerned, in particular foreign policy, economic co-operation, and immigration and asylum policy. A main aim of this co-ordination was 'the reduction of migratory movements into the member states'.[51]

A 1994 Communication from the Commission also called for the EU to take action to address root causes.[52] It identified the different kinds of people on the move: refugees, other persons in need of international protection, and people involved in other migratory movements, suggesting different policy responses to each. Uniquely it recognised that refugees arriving in the EU can themselves be an important source of information on the developing human rights / political situation in their countries of origin. It is regrettable that this concept was never applied in actual practice, because it offered a chance to involve refugees themselves – the primary stakeholders – in improving the quality of information and implementation.

The tide turned with the 1998 Austrian 'Strategy Paper' on asylum and migration policy.[53] This shifted the focus towards preventing the means to immigrate to the EU from countries of transit. The Austrian plan included some highly controversial measures which threatened to undermine refugee protection and development co-operation, yet which were to become recurrent themes in the European asylum debate. These included supplementing, amending, or replacing the 1951 Refugee Convention because it had become 'less relevant' in the changed geo-political climate; making economic aid to third countries dependent on co-operation in migration-management activities; and possible military intervention to prevent migratory flows. The Paper argued that the EU should concentrate on taking action in areas close to Europe, where its influence is greater. In practice, this would mean focusing activity on countries of transit, rather than on countries of origin.

The paper was widely criticised by UNHCR, NGOs, and even some EU governments. In response, the Austrian Presidency produced a second draft, wherein some of the more controversial proposals were modified. Nonetheless, many of the ideas and premises underlying this Strategy Paper have remained influential. The idea of making economic aid to third countries conditional on co-operation in migration management, for example, was revived at the Seville European Council in 2002. Also, the call for countries of transit to create a buffer zone around the EU has been echoed in the proposals to set up Transit Processing Centres in Libya and Tunisia (see Chapter 6).

The Seville European Council in 2002 consolidated the general trend, emphasising the need to address the root causes of *illegal* immigration, and making little reference to human rights. In contrast with Tampere, the Seville Council was interested less in addressing the root causes of refugee flows than in stopping irregular migration to the EU. Seville seemed to view refugee movements as simply another type of illegal immigration.

Developments since Seville: minimal attention to root causes

The Seville Council seemed to view refugee movements as simply another type of illegal immigration.

Although UNHCR's Agenda for Protection calls on states to give greater priority to dealing with root causes of refugee flows, this issue has largely disappeared from the recent EU asylum agenda. Justice and Home Affairs (JHA) priorities currently focus, as we have seen, on interventions to deal with the 'orderly entry' or 'migration management' of asylum seekers, emphasising measures in countries of transit to control onward movement, rather than measures in countries of origin to address the root causes.

This reflects the underlying priority of DG JHA, whose stated objective is to create an 'Area of Freedom Security and Justice' (AFSJ) *within* the Union.[54] It appears to be the view of member states and EU policy makers, almost without exception, that creating an AFSJ within the EU requires limiting the number of illegal immigrants and asylum seekers who arrive and remain within the EU. This basic assumption influences virtually every aspect of the EU's externalised asylum policy. It seems that, so long as the concerns of JHA dominate a supposed 'cross-pillar' approach to asylum and migration, migration-management initiatives will be accorded more attention than projects specifically aimed at addressing the root causes of forced migration.

An example of policy incoherence: the High Level Working Group

In late 1998, in response to a revised draft of the Austrian Paper, the Netherlands proposed a horizontal task force on asylum and migration, charged with developing an integrated, cross-pillar approach to target the situation in countries of origin.[55] The High Level Working Group on Migration and Asylum (HLWG) was officially established in December 1998. It selected six national / regional caseloads to be the focus of 'action plans': Afghanistan / Pakistan; Albania and neighbouring regions; Morocco; Somalia; Sri Lanka; and Iraq. Its cross-policy actions plans would comprise initiatives from a spectrum of EU policy areas and would include a joint analysis of the causes of influx, together with proposals for strengthening common development strategies; identifying and meeting humanitarian needs; and intensifying political and diplomatic dialogue. There would also be a focus on readmission agreements; the possibilities of reception and protection in the region, as well as safe return and repatriation;

and information on co-operation with government organisations, as well as international organisations and NGOs in the region, including UNHCR.[56]

The Action Plans completed are, effectively, compilations of data on asylum and immigration matters in each region, and the third countries' relations with the EU. The Plans contained few, if any, proposals for new, practical steps which the EU could take to address root causes in the regions in question. The analysis contained within the Action Plans was generally consistent with that of international and non-government organisations. However, the Action Plans fail to suggest concrete measures to address these serious concerns about human rights. If anything, the measures proposed in the Action Plans focus on ways to control and even prevent migration from these countries into the EU.

When the Action Plans did propose measures to address human rights and political issues, they tended to be extremely vague, without detailed plans for implementation. This incoherence reflects the fundamental difficulty of co-ordinating EU action across a range of Directorates with differing, and sometimes conflicting, objectives in the field of migration. At the Nice Council in December 2000, the High Level Working Group itself described 'the difficulty of integrating objectives relating to migration into development policies'.[57]

The European Parliament concluded that 'the action plans drawn up by the Group neither make a real political contribution nor do they bring any Community added value to the solution of the problems which remain the root cause of immigration and asylum-seeking'.[58] Containment measures were given far more emphasis than long-term measures to address political and human-rights issues. This reflects the composition of the HLWG, which consisted primarily of officials from member states' ministries of justice or home affairs.[59] While JHA priorities were clearly formulated, therefore, those measures that would normally fall with the competence of DG Relex, such as peace keeping and development assistance, were insubstantial.

The failure of the HLWG to address root causes effectively can also be traced to insufficient transparency and consultation either with civil society or with the countries in question. The first reports of the HLWG were actually drafted without direct dialogue with the countries concerned. The HLWG cited in its defence political and diplomatic considerations: Iraq and Afghanistan, at the time, were isolated internationally and subject to sanctions, while Somalia had no real functioning government.

When it came to potential implementation of the Action Plans, however, the HLWG made more of an effort to incorporate the views of those working directly in the countries concerned. Between 1999 and 2000, the HLWG requested up-dated country assessments from member-state embassies and/or Commission delegations. On the basis of this information, a 'package of measures' was to be implemented in 2000. This move to involve field-based actors was a welcome attempt to enable some 'internationalised' aspects of EU asylum and migration policy to be informed, at least partly, by field-based knowledge. Unfortunately, many of the actions identified for implementation in 2000 were deferred on account of a lack of funding.

Recent developments
The work of the HLWG effectively stalled between 2000 and 2002. Successive EU presidencies discussed the remit and the future of the HLWG, but these discussions had little

concrete impact: there was no successful attempt to provide adequate funding for the Action Plans, nor were any new Plans attempted, nor were the existing Plans updated (notwithstanding changing circumstances in Afghanistan and Iraq, in particular).

The mandate of the HLWG was modified in 2002.[60] The Group was asked to 'promote the EU's role in the efforts of the international community aimed at addressing the main causes for migration', and it was charged with analysing and monitoring migratory trends, and proposing measures to manage migratory flows. The group has also been given a broader geographical remit, and has been encouraged to enhance co-operation with international organisations, including UNHCR and IOM. The HLWG is also charged with analysing the possible links between migration and other policies of the EU.

At the same time, the HLWG is asked to focus on the possibility of concluding more readmission agreements with third countries and improving protection capacity in regions of origin, to analyse the possibilities for safe return and 'internal settlement alternatives', and to propose measures for greater police co-operation in the fight against illegal immigration. It is no longer charged with developing specific Action Plans for specific countries. Instead, it has been functioning recently as a forum to bring together representatives of the Commission and member states from a range of policy areas. It has recently functioned as a forum for discussion between EU policy makers on increasing protection capacity in regions of origin, and also on developing the EU's Neighbourhood Policy.

Measures intended to combat terrorism often have the effect of constraining the rights of asylum seekers arriving in the EU

The impact of increased security concerns

The heightened concerns about security and terrorism in the wake of the events of September 11th 2001 have further complicated efforts to uphold refugee-protection principles. Unfortunately, it appears that measures intended to combat terrorism often have the effect of constraining the rights of asylum seekers arriving in the EU.[61] This problem is exacerbated by the absence of legal means for asylum seekers to obtain protection in the EU. Stringent border controls and interception measures have increased the reliance on people smugglers and traffickers, thereby bringing asylum seekers into a criminalised environment.

It is also true that increased security concerns in the EU are having a negative impact on development co-operation with third countries. At the Seville European Council in 2002, EU leaders decided, in spite of earlier commitments made in the Treaty on European Union, that development policy would not be given an independent role in foreign policy; instead it would be considered together with issues of security, defence, and trade.[62] A European Parliament report has expressed concern that this 'creates a risk of development considerations being seen as less important, even ignored'.[63]

It also appears that, partly because of increased security concerns, ever-greater proportions of EU external funds are being directed towards regions bordering the Union. Even if the development needs of far-off regions may be significantly greater, a concern to broaden EU markets and create stability among the 'near neighbours' means that the EU focus is on creating 'buffer zones' in the CFSP context (similar to those being developed for asylum and migration).[64]

A need for cross-pillar information sharing, but not decision making?

In December 2003, the UN Secretary General launched a Global Commission on International Migration (GCIM). The approach of GCIM is relevant to an EU 'comprehensive approach' to asylum and migration. It acknowledges that, even if national policies on migration are guided primarily by national interest, these policies may have wide repercussions in states and regions beyond the countries directly concerned.[65] The GCIM seeks not only to place migration firmly on the global agenda, but also to explore the links between migration and other issues, including economic development, trade, human rights, poverty alleviation, and national and international security. A clear understanding of these links is of fundamental importance if the EU is indeed to pursue a 'comprehensive approach' to asylum and migration.

In this sense, coherence and co-operation must be the guiding principles for joined-up EU policy on root causes. It is unrealistic and undesirable to expect policy makers whose experience relates (for example) to domestic asylum procedures or border controls to develop innovative projects for overseas development. Past experience, such as that of the HLWG, also shows that differing motivations, and competition for funds, undermine the impact of cross-pillar policy-making.

Instead, there is a real need for cross-pillar and cross-border information sharing. This would involve, firstly, consultation among policy makers based within the EU. Given the focus on an 'externalised asylum agenda', it is also essential that EU policy makers seek and receive information from field-based actors (UN staff, EU staff, NGOs, etc.) regarding the impact of EU external policies on refugee realities on the ground.

Box 12 Addressing root causes of conflict and forced displacement in Sri Lanka

The situation in Sri Lanka shows how multiple, complementary interventions are needed at the political and civil-society levels to build peace. EC actions in development, humanitarian assistance, human rights, and governance all have a part to play. However, these policy areas are not informing EU action on 'migration management' in Sri Lanka.

Sri Lanka is a multi-ethnic and multi-religious country, with (majority Hindu) Tamils (18 per cent of the population) predominating in the northern part, and (majority Buddhist) Sinhalese (74 per cent of the population) in the south and west.[66] The Eastern Province, where most inter-communal conflict occurs today, contains a mix of Muslims, Tamils, and Sinhalese.

The perceived dominance of Tamils under British rule led to a backlash among the rural Sinhalese. After independence in 1948, a series of government policies on language, education, and religion, together with active attempts to change the demographic composition of the country, contributed to an overwhelming sense of marginalisation among ordinary Tamils.[67] While some policies have been redressed, some remain, and Tamils still feel that they are unrepresented and discriminated against.[68]

The prominent Muslim community resisted the concept of a Tamil homeland in the north and east, and allied itself with the Sinhalese security forces. This co-operation led to attacks by the Liberation Tigers of Tamil Eelam (LTTE) on Muslim villages, and *vice versa*, a pattern which manifests itself in the *hartals*, or riots, of today.

Tamil demands for greater autonomy began in the 1930s, and indeed devolved structures were agreed upon in the 1950s and 1960s.[69] But the failure of the government to honour these compromises led many Tamils to conclude that they had no choice but to pursue independence through armed rebellion. The LTTE gained prominence after assassinations of police officers in 1978. A series of massacres by both parties ensued. In the late 1980s, an Indian Peace Keeping Force (IPKF) was invited by the Sri Lankan government to 'hold the peace' in the northern part of the country. The IPKF withdrew after only two years, having sustained significant casualties at the hands of the LTTE. After this time, LTTE consolidated its hold on much of the north, expelling Muslims from their homes in LTTE-controlled areas in 1990 and consolidating (by elimination of much of the rival Tamil Group leadership) their self-proclaimed position as sole representatives of the Tamil people and their aspirations.

The EU in Sri Lanka

For 2003/4, the EC allocated €61.32 million to address humanitarian and development needs in Sri Lanka.[70] As an EU official in Colombo told us, '*Our development programming is what keeps the LTTE at the [negotiating] table*'. Again, as in the DRC, the EC's stated objectives are to support key aspects of the peace process and boost public confidence in transition. The Commission released extra funds (approximately €50,000,000 in 2003/4) for reconstruction of war-affected areas in the north and east.[71] This amount includes €28,500,000 for rural development and €5,300,000 for economic co-operation.[72] As of 12 January 2005, in the wake of the tsunami disaster, ECHO has budgeted €10 million for humanitarian relief in Sri Lanka and the Maldives.[73]

Nine million euro have been channelled through the Aid to Uprooted People budget line to provide health care, education, mine-awareness education, water, sanitation, shelter, and food security to displaced populations.[74] In addition, the Rapid Reaction Mechanism was used in 2002 and 2003 (producing €1,800,000 million and €3,270,000 million, respectively) to fund peace-building initiatives.[75] These included, among other things, support to the Sri Lanka Monitoring Mission (SLMM), the rehabilitation of electricity lines along the Kandy–Jaffna road to facilitate transport through former conflict zones, and funds for the Peace Secretariat to disseminate information to the public and other stakeholders.

ECHO covers Sri Lanka from its regional office in New Delhi. Since the ceasefire agreement, it has invested €22,450,000 in northern Sri Lanka and Tamil Nadu state.[76] Priority areas of assistance include mine-risk education; humanitarian assistance for the Tamil refugees in India and IDPs in welfare centres; and support for the reintegration of new returnees.

Other areas of EU intervention included de-mining (€3,000,000 in 2003), human rights (€5,000,000), and migration co-operation (€2,000,000 since 2001, see below).[77] The EU was also a co-chair of the Tokyo Conference on Reconstruction and Development of Sri Lanka, where the international community pledged $4.5 billion to assist with the country's recovery.[78]

In addition to 'hard' inputs which increase dividends for peace, the EU deployed a mission to observe the parliamentary elections on 2 April 2004. According to the press release issued at the time, this intervention aimed to 'enhance transparency and confidence in the election process' and 'defuse potential tension'.[79] The EU has criticised on-going recruitment and political assassinations in the north and east, both independently and as a co-chair of the Tokyo Conference.

Peace-building initiatives are needed at the local level as well as the national level if a sustainable peace is to be achieved. As analysts have noted: 'If there is a unifying ideology, it is the belief that peace cannot come about purely through political negotiations at the elite level [..]. Society as a whole has to be "prepared" for peace.'[80]

Many NGOs, including Oxfam, therefore support local peace committees who promote mutual tolerance among different ethnic groups. Through recreation and education, Tamils, Muslims, and Sinhalese meet, discuss differences, and ultimately, it is hoped, develop mutual tolerance, which spreads through society at large. On a day-to-day basis, committee members are frequently involved in mediating in local inter-group disputes. In the east, it is common for a single incident such as the theft of a bullock cart to escalate quickly into a generalised riot. Local peace committees help people to separate facts from rumour, and they provide forums for mediation.

In addition to stand-alone activities, conflict-sensitive programming can produce positive dividends for peace. Specialised analyses can help organisations to 'do no harm' as well as maximise opportunities to build trust among groups. In Sri Lanka, many agencies integrate Peace and Conflict Impact Assessment[81] into their programme design. Of course, for the peace to be truly sustainable, sensitivity to conflict must guide the EU and donor governments' overall strategy towards Sri Lanka. One observer noted the fact that Western countries fund UNICEF while training government armed forces: '*Western governments' support to the Sri Lankan military undermines the LTTE's confidence*', causing it to intensify its recruitment activities. '*The bottom line*', he suggested, '*is always to consider the impact of your actions on people at the grass roots.*'

Recommendations

Principles

- EU leaders should respond to the call in UNHCR's Agenda for Protection, to give greater priority to addressing the root causes of refugee movements. This response should focus not merely on the causes of secondary movements to the EU, but on the causes of forced migration from countries of origin. Root causes need to be explicitly investigated by the EU, so that specific objectives can be planned and monitored.
- Legitimate security concerns should not lead to the diluting of refugee-protection principles by EU member states; nor should they lead to the diversion of much-needed EU development funds from (far-off) regions to regions bordering the EU.

Application

- An EU response to dealing with root causes requires co-ordinated action across external policy areas, including development, humanitarian assistance, external relations, and CFSP. Rather than cross-pillar *policy making* in a politicised context driven by home-affairs concerns, on the model of the HLWG, EU policy makers within each of these areas must incorporate cross-pillar *information sharing* at all stages of project development and implementation.
- For this purpose, the High Level Working Group, in its current form, could perform a useful function; i.e. serving not as a body for policy making, but as a forum within which policy makers and stakeholders from a range of policy areas can share information.
- In addition to co-ordination within Brussels, it is important for EU policy makers to incorporate the expertise of stakeholders in the countries in question, to assess need, guide implementation, and monitor impact of EU actions on root causes of refugee situations. In particular, mid-term review of CSPs should be a transparent process, involving inputs from civil society not only in the ACP countries, where it is mandated, but in all countries. Serious consideration should also be given to the proposal made by the Commission in 1994: to see refugees themselves as a potential source of information on their countries of origin.

Summary of recommendations

To ensure that EU actions respect the rights and promote the safety of asylum seekers, and that they positively contribute to a global system to ensure protection and find solutions for refugees, Oxfam notes the following principles and makes the following recommendations.

1. On EU territory : decisions about safety elsewhere

Oxfam notes that:

Asylum seekers have the right to have their claims individually examined by means of a full and fair procedure. This should be the cornerstone of EU asylum policy, regardless of asylum seekers' country of origin and/or transit and their method of entry to the EU.

No country can be considered safe for all of its citizens. EU lists of safe countries should not be drawn up. Non-state agents cannot guarantee to fulfil the duties of a state, and should not be considered as realistic sources of effective, durable protection from persecution.

Oxfam therefore recommends that:

When transposing the Directives of the first stage of the Common European Asylum System (CEAS), **EU member states** must strive to exceed minimum standards and meet their commitment, made at the meeting of the European Council in Tampere in 1999, to fully respect and fulfil their international obligations. On no account should they lower their existing standards towards the minimum. In developing the second stage of the CEAS, EU member states must meet the commitment made in The Hague Programme to a 'full and inclusive application of the Geneva Convention on Refugees and other relevant treaties'.

EU policy makers in each institution should establish a more structured and transparent approach to consultation on asylum, involving independent experts, including NGOs and UNHCR. In particular the **Council of the EU** should create a framework for consultation; the **Commission** should formalise current forums; and the **European Parliament** should continue to undertake meaningful dialogue with stakeholder groups.

In the short term, the **Commission** should increase the transparency of EURASIL meetings, to allow information to be shared between member states and independent experts. In the medium to long term, **EU leaders** should explore the possibility of establishing an independent Country of Origin Information (COI) documentation centre, with adequate resources to ensure accurate and up-to-date information. This measure should be accompanied by a mechanism for independent scrutiny of COI. High quality of COI must be accompanied by high-quality training of immigration officials, to ensure that the information is used to make sound decisions in asylum cases.

International, national, and local agencies in countries of origin should continue efforts to streamline the monitoring and communication of human-rights violations. **EU and member-state delegations** should create forums in which these agencies, as well as affected individuals, can channel current and accurate information to European COI mechanisms.

2. On the edges of the EU: 'managing migration' from Europe's neighbours

Controlling access: borders, barriers, and interception

Oxfam notes that:

A central principle of international law is that of non-refoulement. This means that asylum seekers must not be turned away from EU territory, or prevented from accessing that territory in the first place, without an adequate assessment of their protection needs taking place.

Responsibility stems from the actions of states, wherever these actions occur. Therefore EU member states' immigration-control measures must be in line with the obligation to uphold the right to seek asylum.

Oxfam therefore recommends that:

EU member states must ensure that immigration-control measures contain effective safeguards for differentiating between persons in need of international protection and other migrants. These safeguards must include mechanisms to assess the asylum cases of people claiming to be in need of international protection. Such assessments must be carried out by qualified personnel.

EU policy makers should meet their objective of creating more and appropriate legal migration channels, as part of a comprehensive immigration and asylum policy.

Securing the co-operation of transit countries

Oxfam notes that:

Migration-management concerns must not dominate or dictate EU relationships with third countries. In particular, development co-operation should never be made conditional on co-operation in 'migration management'; and migration-management concerns must not detract from EU action to promote human rights and democratisation in third countries.

Oxfam therefore recommends that:

States signing EU Neighbourhood or Readmission agreements, or other EU or bilateral 'migration management' agreements, must guarantee to protect and not to refoule people who are transferred to their territory.

The EU and its member states should avoid concluding readmission agreements, or other 'migration management' agreements, with countries which have inadequate asylum systems, which are not signatories to the 1951 Convention, and/or which have poor human-rights records.

In agreeing readmission agreements, the **EU and member states** should elicit meaningful guarantees from third countries on the treatment of migrants returned there.

In implementing the European Neighbourhood Policy (ENP), **EU leaders** should emphasise not merely migration management, but also the need to strengthen the refugee-protection capacities of the third countries concerned. Those ENP countries that have not acceded to the 1951 Convention, and/or to other major human-rights instruments, should be encouraged to do so.

EU leaders and third countries should commit themselves to monitoring and evaluating the protection impact of migration-management activities, in particular on returned asylum seekers.

3. In regions of refugee origin: promoting 'orderly entry'

Oxfam notes that:

EU resettlement schemes or other 'orderly entry' measures must be complementary to, not a replacement for, a full and fair system for dealing with spontaneous arrivals of asylum seekers on EU territory. Resettlement must be viewed as a tool for providing international protection and durable solutions for selected refugees, and not as a tool of migration management. Any distinctions between 'good' resettled refugees and 'bad' spontaneous arrivals must be avoided, in rhetoric and in practice.

Within this context, member states should be encouraged to expand their resettlement activity; first within a guiding EU framework, and subsequently as part of a more coherent EU-wide resettlement scheme.

Oxfam therefore recommends that:

EU member states should continue the European tradition of conducting resettlement on the basis of vulnerability and need for protection, not merely on the basis of links and prospects for integration.

The implementation of resettlement schemes should be properly resourced, in order to operate effectively and not detract from protection activities. **EU member states** should draw on and involve the experience and knowledge of UNHCR and NGOs in operating resettlement schemes, as well as dialogue with stakeholders in the country and region.

If **member states** are unwilling to operate Protected Entry Procedures, they should be encouraged not to place obstructive visa restrictions on nationals from countries where human-rights violations are widespread.

4. In regions of origin: enhancing protection or exporting asylum?

Oxfam notes that :

Transit Processing Centres should not be established, because they would amount to shifting the burden of caring for Europe's refugees on to poor countries which could not guarantee their safety.

EU efforts to increase protection capacity in regions of origin could make a positive contribution to international refugee protection, and could be concrete acts of responsibility sharing.

However, Regional Protection Programmes (RPPs) must not be used as bargaining chips by the EU to encourage third countries to co-operate in managing migration, or to accept returns, particularly of third-country nationals. Member states' support for RPPs should not be contingent on short-term migration-management goals which are unlikely to be met.

Countries hosting refugee populations have a responsibility for the realisation of refugees' full rights within their available resources, and with international assistance where necessary. Refugees should not be treated as scapegoats for political ends, nor unnecessarily warehoused in refugee camps and so denied the opportunity of local integration.

Oxfam therefore recommends that:

RPPs should comprise well-resourced, long-term initiatives which are targeted according to an assessment of real protection needs in the regions and countries in question, based on a full and inclusive interpretation of effective protection. However, at this stage, much greater clarity is required about the aims, contents, and resourcing of RPPs. The **European Commission** must ensure that their development, future implementation, and evaluation is based on transparent dialogue with **stakeholders in the region** (refugee communities, UNHCR, NGOs, and governments), as well as on policy coherence with existing EU development and humanitarian activities in the regions/countries.

Governments in the region must ensure that protection of refugees, as well as the welfare of the host communities, is accorded paramount importance in this dialogue with the EU, above political or financial gains.

5: Countries of origin: the root causes of refugee flows

The impact of EU external policy actions

Oxfam notes that :

Policy coherence is necessary to ensure that EU external actions address rather than exacerbate forced migration, and that the home-affairs migration-management actions are not at odds with human rights, development, and humanitarian objectives.

Oxfam therefore recommends that:

In implementing aspects of the 'internationalised' asylum agenda, **EU policy makers** should take advantage of pre-existing channels of communication and forums that have been established in other areas of EU policy (in the context of the Cotonou Agreement, for example).

EU asylum policy makers should draw on the experience of ECHO and seek to combine a bottom–up view with a top–down approach to ensure that projects are chosen and implemented according to the need for protection.

Targeted development assistance can make an essential contribution to the design of durable solutions, supporting host communities and reducing displacement in the long term.
EU member states must ensure that development assistance is not made conditional on 'migration management' co-operation.

EU member states must respect their international humanitarian and human-rights responsibilities if engaging in the supply of arms; must adequately assess the potential impact of their arms exports on volatile situations; and must seek agreement on an International Arms Trade Treaty, to control arms in a way that will safeguard sustainable development and human rights.

Coherence or co-operation? Joined-up EU policy

Oxfam notes that:

EU leaders should respond to the call expressed in UNHCR's Agenda for Protection, to give greater priority to addressing the root causes of refugee movements. This response should focus not merely on the causes of secondary movements to the EU, but on the causes of forced migration from countries of origin. Root causes need to be explicitly mapped by the EU so that specific objectives can be planned and monitored.

Legitimate security concerns should not lead to the diluting of refugee-protection principles by EU member states, nor should they lead to the diversion of much-needed EU development funds from (far-off) regions to regions bordering the EU.

Oxfam therefore recommends that:

An EU response to dealing with root causes requires co-ordinated action across external policy areas, including development, humanitarian assistance, external relations, and Common Foreign and Security Policy (CFSP). Rather than cross-pillar *policy making* in a politicised context driven by home-affairs concerns, on the model of the High Level Working Group, **EU policy makers** within each of these areas must incorporate cross-pillar *information sharing* at all stages of project development and implementation.

For this purpose, the **High Level Working Group**, in its current form, could perform a useful function; i.e. not as a body for policy making, but as a forum within which policy makers and stakeholders from a range of policy areas can share information.

In addition to co-ordination within Brussels, it is important that **EU policy makers** incorporate the expertise of stakeholders in the countries in question, to assess need, guide implementation, and monitor impact of EU actions on root causes of refugee situations. In particular, mid-term review of Country Strategy Papers should be a transparent process, involving **inputs from civil society** not only in the African, Caribbean, and Pacific group of countries, where it is mandatory, but in all countries. Serious consideration should also be given to the proposal made by the Commission in 1994: to see **refugees themselves** as a potential source of information on their countries of origin.

Annex 1: Profile of Sri Lanka

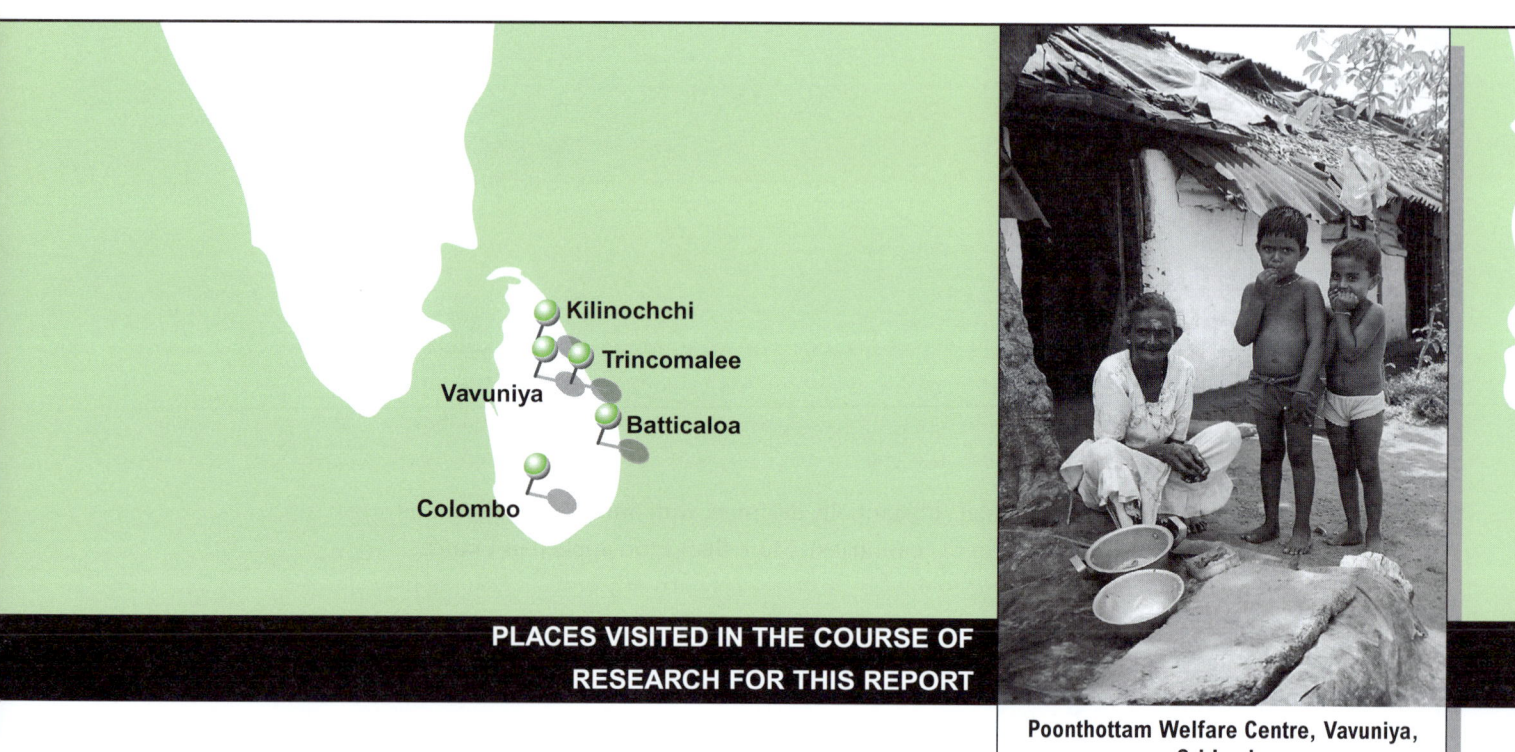

Poonthottam Welfare Centre, Vavuniya, Sri Lanka
© Jessica Schultz

Political background

'The absence of war does not mean peace.'
Donor, Colombo

More than 20 years of civil war in Sri Lanka have cost at least 64,000 lives and displaced nearly one million people.[1] In December 2001, the political factors that had obstructed progress in previous negotiations diminished in significance after the pro-peace UNP triumphed in parliamentary elections. Three months later, Sri Lankan Prime Minister Ranil Wickremasinghe and Veelupillai Prabharakan, leader of the Liberation Tigers of Tamil Eelam (LTTE), signed a Memorandum of Understanding, building on a unilateral ceasefire by the LTTE in December 2001, which was quickly matched by the new government. Both the government security forces and the Tigers agreed to cease military action, including assassinations and abductions and prohibited acts against the civilian population. Such acts included 'torture, intimidation, abduction, extortion and harassment'.[2] The Norwegian-led Sri Lanka Monitoring Mission (SLMM) was established to oversee compliance with the accord.

Formal peace talks began, facilitated by the Norwegian government, in September 2002 in Thailand. Five more rounds followed, covering issues ranging from power sharing and rehabilitation needs in war-affected areas to resettlement of IDPs. However, in April 2003 the LTTE unilaterally suspended their involvement in the talks, claiming that the government had failed to deliver on critical promises to rebuild devastated Tamil areas and move out of High Security Zones in Jaffna.[3] They also resented the fact that they had not been invited to a high-profile donor meeting hosted by the US government in Washington. Since then, the ceasefire has been observed, but the future of the peace process is unclear.

Forced displacement: facts and figures

The major movement of Sri Lankans into Europe, Canada, and elsewhere began when fighting flared up in 1983. By 2002, 122,351 Sri Lankan nationals had been granted refugee status worldwide.[4] Of these, 64,000 live in India, and the majority of the others reside in France, Canada, and the UK.[5] About 90 per cent of all migrants from Sri Lanka are Tamil; the asylum seekers claimed that they faced persecution from the Sri Lankan security forces or forced recruitment by the LTTE.[6]

Since the ceasefire was signed in 2002, the number of Sri Lankans seeking asylum in the 29 industrialised countries of the world has decreased. In 2002, Sri Lankans comprised the ninth-largest group of asylum seekers worldwide. Of 10,158 applications, 7519 were submitted within the EU. Of these, nearly half were lodged in the UK.[7]

However, by the end of 2003 numbers had substantially declined, with only 5441 applications made in industrialised countries (3098 in EU countries). More than 1700 applied in France, and 1200 in Canada. In terms of migrants to the EU, Sri Lanka is currently only 24th on the list of countries of origin.[8] According to some sources, the actual numbers of Sri Lankans coming to Europe have probably not dropped as dramatically as this fact suggests. 'Hidden migration' continues, but since the ceasefire people are less likely to claim asylum to regularise their status.

Sri Lankan refugees in India

Most Sri Lankans in need of protection lack the means to leave their country. Of those who do, the majority get as far as Tamil Nadu in India, where approximately 61,000 refugees currently live in 103 refugee camps. Another 20,000 refugees are displaced outside the camps in local communities nearby.[9] Although India recognises the Sri Lankans as *de facto* refugees, India is not a party to the UN Refugee Convention and has no national legislation regarding refugees. The Sri Lankans in camps receive food rations and minimal cash assistance, as well as space to build homes. Children are permitted to attend local Indian schools. However, water and sanitation are inadequate in many of the camps, and freedom of movement is severely restricted. Neither UNHCR nor international NGOs are permitted access to refugees in the camps in India.

UNHCR–Sri Lanka facilitates 'priority' returns of refugees from Tamil Nadu. Its activities include interviews to verify the voluntary nature of return, and co-ordination of logistical arrangements with Sri Lankan and Indian authorities. Although most communities welcome the returnees, some observers note that the situation is not entirely secure. *'In the Vanni the LTTE have an eye on them'*, said one service provider. Returnees are sometimes suspected of links to the Indian intelligence units, especially men who come on their own.[10]

Sri Lankan IDPs

The vast majority of the displaced remain within the borders of Sri Lanka. Primary responsibility for assistance and protection lies with the Sri Lankan government, which co-ordinates support to internally displaced people through its Ministry of Relief, Rehabilitation, and Reconciliation. UNHCR's complementary mandate was first endorsed by the UN Secretary General in 1991. Today, its programme aims to address the emergency humanitarian needs of spontaneous returnees, facilitate preparations for the voluntary returns of refugees, and strengthen the capacity of the government and national NGOs to answer protection and humanitarian needs of the displaced. To this end, it has established district-level 'protection networks' with the Danish Refugee Council and two national bodies, the Human Rights Commission and the Legal Aid Foundation. Much of their work concerns rights awareness, documentation, and mediation in property disputes. UNHCR also monitors returning refugees from India in Mannar and Jaffna and evaluates whether or not in-country returns are voluntary.

Refugees in Sri Lanka

As Sri Lanka is not party to the 1951 Geneva Convention, UNHCR staff determine the status of individuals who claim asylum in the country. As one official from the Ministry of Foreign Affairs explains, *'As a national policy, we don't encourage refugees. We have our own problems to address. With the ethnic conflict here, refugees pose a serious security threat.'* UNHCR relies on referrals from immigration officers at the airport and embassies to identify most of its small caseload (around 40 persons in June 2004, mainly from Iraq and Afghanistan).[11] Because refugees are not allowed to work, or receive free health care or education, the UNHCR supports everyone under its mandate in Colombo, while pursuing third-country resettlement options.

Access to asylum in Sri Lanka is further constrained by recently intensified efforts to combat illegal migration. The increasing number of individuals being smuggled through Sri Lanka has caused concern in countries which consider themselves potential endpoints. The United Kingdom, Canada, and India have all applied pressure on the Sri Lankan government to adopt strong immigration legislation to prevent onward movement. The government itself claims that smuggling networks have links to terrorism (LTTE) and drugs.[12] To control its borders better, therefore, the Sri Lankan government has drafted a revised Immigration and Emigration Act which imposes greater penalties on traffickers and strict removal procedures for certain non-citizens. The Act contains no provisions to protect victims of trafficking, including refugees, and effectively allows refoulement, with no recourse to the courts. As the UNHCR points out, *'it's a law that punishes victims and perpetrators indiscriminately'*.[13]

The EU in Sri Lanka

The European Commission and Sri Lanka have a long history of formal co-operation, beginning with their first bilateral agreement in 1975. This co-operation has traditionally focused on poverty alleviation through rural development. In 1995, the Commission opened its delegation in Colombo. As of 12 January 2005, in the wake of the tsunami, ECHO has budgeted €10 million for Sri Lanka and the Maldives.[14] For 2003–2004, the EC allocated €61.32 million to address humanitarian and development needs in Sri Lanka. Strategy is designed in Brussels, based on country visits and communications with staff in the field. With the exception of two budget lines (Rehabilitation and Aid to Uprooted People), most funding decisions are made from Brussels, based on recommendations put forward by the Delegation.[15] Decisions on migration co-operation are especially centralised. As Delegation staff explained, in initiatives related to Justice et Affaires Intérieures *'the role of the delegation is nul'*.

Co-operation for migration management

In 1999, the High-Level Working Group produced an Action Plan for migration co-operation between Sri Lanka and the EU. This plan included an analysis of the causes of flight, and set forth a series of actions required by the EC/EU in the fields of foreign policy, development and economic co-operation, and migration. These ranged from the extremely general ('contribute to as rapid as possible reduction of the level of poverty in Sri Lanka') to the specific ('organize an information campaign to warn against the consequences of illegally entering EU member states').[16] One recommendation – to enter into a formal agreement to facilitate the orderly return from the EU to Sri Lanka of Sri Lankans found residing illegally in the EU – came to fruition on 4 June 2004.[17] The EU Readmission Agreement was scheduled to take effect in early or mid-2005.

Since its establishment, the EC's migration co-operation budget has financed two organisations for work in Sri Lanka. One, the International Organisation for Migration (IOM), received funds for a project to reduce irregular migration into and through Sri Lanka. The three components included (a) training immigration officials to detect document fraud, undertake risk-profiling of migrants, and identify/handle potential trafficking victims; (b) providing support to the Bureau of Foreign Employment to disseminate information for out-going migrants; and (c) assisting voluntary returns.[18] In 2003, IOM received additional AENEAS funds (€1,060,000), to continue most of its current work.[19]

The second beneficiary of migration co-operation funds in Sri Lanka is the International Centre for Migration Policy Development (ICMPD). This Vienna-based organisation received a grant of €1,100,000 in early 2002 to establish the Source Country Information Systems–Sri Lanka (SCIS). This project aimed to assist the European Community with return implementation and asylum determinations by providing case-specific information on countries of origin upon request to member-state governments.[20] Despite the recent conclusion of a Readmission Agreement between the EU and Sri Lanka, the ICMPD project funding will not be renewed.[21]

Oxfam's work in Sri Lanka

The tsunami disaster which struck the Indian Ocean region on 26 December 2004 has led to further displacement in Sri Lanka, with more than 800,000 survivors living in temporary camps or with friends and relatives. Oxfam is responding with both emergency and rehabilitation work in five locations, and extending its reach into the south of the country. At the time of writing (January 2005), Oxfam aims to reach 25,000 affected families directly; many of these will be new beneficiaries. The emergency response programme will quickly become a rehabilitation programme, supplementing and complementing Oxfam's on-going development work in Sri Lanka.

Oxfam GB has worked in Sri Lanka since 1968 and has five offices in the country: one in Colombo, two in the north, and two in the east. Oxfam offices in the east are located in Batticaloa and Trincomalee. Oxfam and its partners work in areas controlled both by the government of Sri Lanka and by the LTTE. The Batticaloa office has a much larger sphere of engagement, reaching down into Ampara, and it runs pioneering conflict-reduction projects. Oxfam is seen as a major player in programme implementation, including micro-credit and livelihoods work, emergency preparedness, and security and protection. Projects whose management has been transferred to local partners cover livelihoods support, humanitarian assistance, and initiatives to end violence against women and to reduce conflict.

Oxfam's offices in the north are located in Kilinochchi and Vavuniya (covering Vavuniya and Mannar districts). The area covered by the Kilinochchi office is situated in what can be regarded as the administrative capital of the LTTE-controlled areas. Both Mannar and Vavuniya districts are largely under government control, but are right on the forward defence line. The Vavuniya office is operationally involved in camps, known as Welfare Centres, which accommodate internally displaced people. Although these are run by the government, Oxfam maintains the water and sanitation facilities. Welfare Centres have emptied somewhat, thus creating some opportunity to work with those people who have relocated or resettled. Oxfam's presence in the Centres gives it influence on policy making on issues regarding public health, coercion, and food-aid supply.

For this study, the consultant travelled to Colombo, Kilinochchi, Vavuniya, Trincomalee, and Batticaloa. Key informants included war-affected civilians in Poonthottam Welfare Centre (Vavuniya), Magarambaikulm Village (Vavuniya), Sobalapoliyankulam Village (Vavuniya), Wattaram East (Batticaloa), and Nilaveli Welfare Centre (Trincomalee).The consultant also spoke to staff from international and national organisations, government agencies, embassies, and bilateral/multilateral donors: Oxfam GB, UNHCR, UNICEF, ICRC, IOM, ICMPD, UNDP, Asian Development Bank, Nonviolent Peace Force, SLMM, Danish Refugee Council, Asia Foundation, Center for Human Rights and Development, Human Rights Commission of Sri Lanka, Consortium of Humanitarian Agencies, ZOA Refugee Care, FLICT, WUSF, Foundation for Coexistence, SEED, FORUT, CARE, SEDEC (Caritas), Forum for Human Development, Kinnya Vision, Kinnya, The Embassy of Switzerland, the British High Commission, SIDA, DFID, the European Commission, the Dutch Embassy, USAID OTI, the European Commission, the Dutch Embassy, the Sri Lankan Ministry of Public Security, and the Ministry of Foreign Affairs, Law and Order.

Annex 2: Profile of the United Republic of Tanzania

PLACES VISITED IN THE COURSE OF RESEARCH FOR THIS REPORT

Tutsi boy in Lugufu camp, Tanzania
© Jessica Schultz

Forced displacement: facts and figures

Tanzania hosts the largest refugee population in Africa: approximately one million people have fled from consecutive crises in neighbouring countries during the past dozen years. According to UNHCR statistics, there were about 650,000 official refugees in Tanzania at the end of 2003.[22] Many others are not registered but live illegally in towns or fishing villages along Lake Tanganyika. In 2003, UNHCR assisted 480,000 refugees, including 324,200 from Burundi, 150,200 from the DRC, 3300 from Somalia, and 2000 from other countries or of mixed origins.[23] Approximately 50 per cent of assisted refugees are female, and 55 per cent are under 18 years of age.[24] Most are agriculturalists or, in the case of the Congolese, earn their livelihood by fishing. Almost all of the official Congolese refugees live in one of three camps: Nyarugusu in Kasulu District, Lugufu in Kigoma District, and Mkugwa (for so-called 'protection cases' and other non-Burundian refugees) near Kibondo.

'It's better to die from a bullet than to die from hunger.'
Congolese refugee returning home to Uvira

Tanzania is generally not considered to be a transit country for refugees entering Europe. Rather, refugees remain 'warehoused' for years, often decades, in camps with scant opportunity to earn their own income or pursue higher education. According to the Director of the Ministry of Home Affairs Refugee Department, local integration is out of the question: *'Our goal is to see all the refugees go back home'*.

Refugees in Tanzania: new arrivals from the DRC

Most Congolese who seek refuge in Tanzania come from South Kivu province, near Lake Tanganyika. Since a peace agreement was signed in the Democratic Republic of Congo in 2003, the numbers of refugees have declined sharply to 5600, down from 17,000 in 2002.[25] Only 153 refugees had arrived in Kigoma district in the period from January to August 2004.[26] Of the refugees who come through the official channels, most claim to be fleeing individualised persecution in the DRC.

Who becomes a refugee rather than an IDP? According to a UNHCR field officer, *'[Congolese] move from one village to another until they get tired. They realise that peace is not near and decide to cross.'* Some are motivated to move by the relatively good medical care and education provided in the Tanzanian camps. Of those who travel through Tanzania, most move on to neighbouring countries, such as Zambia and Uganda, in search of economic opportunities.

Political background: Tanzania's refugee policy

Tanzania is party to both the 1951 Refugee Convention and the 1969 OAU Convention. The Ministry of Home Affairs and UNHCR co-ordinate assistance, while the Office of the Prime Minister is responsible for the co-ordination of government business and disaster management at the central level. The President's Office oversees the decentralised local government system.

Under the leadership of President Julius Nyerere, Tanzania pursued, in the spirit of pan-Africanism, a liberal open-door policy towards refugees in the 1960s and 1970s. Approximately 190,000 Burundians who came during the 1970s were each given 2.5 hectares to farm and, living in settlements originally established by UNHCR, they have achieved *de facto* integration with the local community.

Tanzania's open attitude towards refugees changed during the 1990s after mass influxes from the Great Lakes region. These refugees were perceived to be more militarised, and they catalysed a general fear, according to one Tanzanian official, that *'if allowed to integrate in Tanzania, they would import the Hutu–Tutsi problem'*. Others suspected that the densely populated countries of Burundi and Rwanda might try to use Tanzania to release some of the pressure on their resources unless the government made it clear that refugees would be returned at the earliest opportunity. In the 1990s, therefore, refugee policy shifted from local integration to temporary protection. Officially, the government cites insecurity, banditry, damage to infrastructure, and environmental degradation as the main threats posed by the presence of refugees. Since the mid-1990s, only a small group of Somalis (approximately 3000) with historic links to Tanzania have been allowed to settle.

Refugees are still theoretically eligible for Tanzanian citizenship on a case-by-case basis. In practice, naturalisation has proved difficult. Cases are often left pending for many years, and most refugees cannot afford the Tsh 650,000 (US$650) that it costs to complete the process.[27] Refugee men with Tanzanian wives are at a particular disadvantage, because the law requires men to prove that they can support their spouse before being granted citizenship.

In 2003, the government of Tanzania signalled its impatience with the *status quo* by drafting a new National Refugee Policy. Echoing proposals in Europe and elsewhere, the Policy, published in September 2003, advocates 'Safe Zones' to be established to process refugees in their countries of origin. It also reiterates the priority placed on repatriation as a durable solution for refugees.[28] Donor fatigue has not helped matters much. Assistance to refugee-hosting areas has tapered off, to the point where authorities, as one informant put it, *'must threaten deportation – then their [the donors'] ears perk up'*. The Ministry of Home Affairs has convened a task force to review the National Refugee Act of 1998 and propose amendments that would harmonise the Act with the National Refugee Policy.

Limitations to Tanzania's refugee-hosting capacity

There are genuine constraints on Tanzania's capacity to provide protection and assistance to refugees on its territory. The government has frequently complained that it must invest scarce resources in the security of the north-west region, rather than improving overall development.[29] It has also criticised the international community for its failure to effectively share the burden of the refugees' presence. In the absence of a mobilised civil society, there is little public sympathy for the rights of refugees.

According to the Tanzania Poverty and Human Development Report for 2002, Tanzania still struggles to meet the basic needs of its own citizens: 'The 1990s have not brought significant net gains in the reduction of income poverty for the majority of the population. Income poverty has only significantly declined in urban areas. While the proportion of people living below the poverty line has decreased, their number has increased.'[30] Thirty-six per cent of the population falls below the basic-needs poverty line, including 39 per cent in rural areas. A quarter of adults have no education, and 29 per cent are considered illiterate. For women, the statistics are even more grim. Forty-one per cent of rural women can neither read nor write. One positive impact of recent development initiatives is the significant increase in primary-school enrolment. When school fees were abolished in 2002, the numbers of children in school increased to 1,659,847 from 894,894 two years earlier.[31]

Hosting such a large refugee population has caused strains and resentments, but has also brought to local residents the significant benefits of renovated schools, hospitals, and roads. In many areas, community members use the better-equipped refugee hospitals instead of their designated district hospitals.[32] UNHCR provides vaccinations and tuberculosis treatment to Tanzanian nationals living near the camps. In addition, numerous primary and secondary schools have been established to benefit both refugee and local children. Environment-remediation programmes have led to extensive reforestation. Finally, access to safe water in refugee-hosting regions is now greater than in many other parts of the country.[33] The team leader of a study assessing the impact of refugee presence in north-western Tanzania indicates that, after the initial destruction and disruption caused by the mass influxes of the mid-1990s, the net impact of refugees has probably shifted from negative to positive. The study's leader notes that the positive benefits are insufficiently acknowledged by authorities. Refugees' advocates and service providers have 'done a terrible PR job with the government'.[34]

Nor are refugees prominent on the agenda of most international donors. According to informants in Dar es Salaam, current priorities include measures to combat terrorism, support for the 2005 general elections, control of HIV/AIDS, and poverty reduction. Most bilateral donors provide budget support through Tanzania's official Poverty Reduction Strategy Programme, which has no particular focus on the refugee-affected regions. DANIDA, exceptionally, funds a Tanzania Refugee Host Areas Programme with several million dollars, and the UNDP has recently initiated a special project for north-west Tanzania to strengthen local capacity for the co-ordination of aid.

The EU in Tanzania

The European Union and its member states provide about €400,000,000 annually in aid to Tanzania.[35] Key donors include Sweden, Denmark, and the United Kingdom. The EC itself focuses on road infrastructure, basic education, good governance, health, HIV/AIDS, and the judiciary. One joint initiative between the Commission and the government of Tanzania, which targeted the north-west and was called Special Programmes for Refugee Affected Areas (SPRAA), ended in August 2003. The purpose of this programme was to improve Tanzania's ability to accommodate refugees from the Great Lakes region, following the influx after the Rwandan genocide. In addition to sectoral support for transport infrastructure, environment-protection projects, and other 'hardware' interventions, it funded a review of national refugee policies by the Centre for the Study of Forced Migration at the University of Dar es Salaam.

Currently, by far the most significant assistance supplied by the EC to refugee communities is channelled through ECHO.[36] For ECHO, Tanzania is prioritised as a 'forgotten emergency' – one with low donor presence and media coverage, among other indicators. ECHO fully funds 50 per cent of UNHCR's programme in all 13 refugee camps in Tanzania – a lifeline of support for a population destined to remain dependent on aid for the foreseeable future.

Oxfam's work in Tanzania

Oxfam GB's programme in Tanzania targets improvements in education, livelihoods, and disaster preparedness and response, and aims to strengthen the underlying processes of accountability. It focuses mainly on the drought-prone areas of northern and north-western Tanzania, working with local government authorities and non-state groups. Oxfam mounted a large-scale response to the mass influxes of refugees in the 1990s, and continued to provide water and sanitation services to a large proportion of camp-bound refugees as well as to local communities. Oxfam transferred responsibility for the schemes to other NGOs in 2001, but continues to support refugee services by seconding an expert water and sanitation co-ordinator to UNHCR, and by helping to increase local emergency-response capacity.

In Tanzania, the consultant conducted interviews in Dar es Salaam, Kigoma town and district, and Lugufu I and II refugee camps. Informants included Congolese refugees, in addition to representatives from UNHCR, ECHO, the Tanzanian Ministry of Home Affairs, the Consulate of the Democratic Republic of the Congo, World Vision, the European Commission Delegation in Tanzania, the Royal Norwegian Embassy, UNICEF, the British High Commission, DFID, Tanganyika Christian Refugee Service, UNDP, and the Centre for the Study of Forced Migration (University of Dar es Salaam).

Annex 3: Profile of The Democratic Republic of Congo

PLACES VISITED IN THE COURSE OF RESEARCH FOR THIS REPORT

Camp Aero, Bunia, Democratic Republic of Congo
© Jane Beesley / Oxfam GB

Political background

'Even with MONUC here, people are afraid.'
Resident, Bunia

The recent wars in the DRC began in 1996 with Rwandan attacks aimed at dislodging refugee camps in Eastern DRC which were being used as staging posts for rebel incursions into Rwanda. The Rwandan offensive against DRC-based rebels was made under the cover of a rebellion led by Laurent Kabila against the dictatorial regime of Mobutu Sese Seku. In May 1997, after capturing Kinshasa with the support of Rwandan and Ugandan forces and causing Mobutu to flee, the rebel leader Laurent Kabila declared himself President and subsequently changed the name of the country from Zaire to the Democratic Republic of Congo.

However, the peace was short-lived. In 1998, as Kabila tried to distance himself from his Rwandan and Ugandan supporters, war broke out again. This second rebellion was launched by the Rwandan-backed Rassemblement Congolais pour la Démocratie (RCD) and by the Ugandan-backed Mouvement pour la Libération du Congo (MLC). A ceasefire agreement was signed in July 1999 and reconfirmed in February 2001, after Laurent Kabila was assassinated and his son Joseph subsequently took power. Representatives from six countries and several rebel groups signed the Lusaka Accord and initiated a peace process known as the Inter-Congolese Dialogue, which also included representatives of Congolese civil society. UN military observers were subsequently deployed to monitor compliance with the ceasefire agreement.

Despite these developments, violence spread in the east, involving various Rwandan and Burundian rebel groups, anti-Kabila forces, and community-based Mayi Mayi militia, backed by the Kinshasa regime. In Ituri, the vicious conflict between the Hema and Lendu inhabitants demonstrated the incapacity of the central government to maintain control in the resource-rich east.

In December 2002 in Pretoria, South Africa, the parties signed the Global and Inclusive Agreement on Transition in the Democratic Republic of the Congo.[37] A power-sharing arrangement retains Joseph Kabila as President and includes four Vice-Presidents from the MLC, RCD–Goma, the Kabila governing clique in Kinshasa, and the political opposition. Many Congolese lack faith in the stability of this structure.[38] Meanwhile, atrocities against civilians continue in parts of Eastern DRC.

Forced displacement: facts and figures

Because of current instability in the DRC, the number of displaced people is exceedingly difficult to measure. UNOCHA estimates that there are 2.3 million IDPs in the DRC, in nine of the country's eleven provinces.[39] Approximately 453,400 Congolese have sought refuge in neighbouring African countries.[40] According to one study, four-fifths of all families in rural areas of North and South Kivu have been displaced at least once during the past five years.[41] Although 1.1 million people have returned home since 2003, between May and August 2004 150,000 individuals were newly uprooted.[42] Only a tiny fraction of them make their way to Europe – mainly to French-speaking countries such as Belgium and France.[43] In all, approximately 9000 applications for asylum were lodged by Congolese nationals in the EU during 2003.[44]

Refugees in the DRC

The DRC itself is home to a large refugee population. Of the approximately 241,000 refugees, most have lived in the country for at least a decade.[45] Some, especially among the Angolans, have resided in the DRC for over twenty-five years. Given the turbulence in the DRC itself, there are no prospects of meaningful integration. As one UNHCR staff member noted, *'transience is a basic characteristic of the population here'*: even the local inhabitants lack security.

Congolese law requires refugees to remain in settlements unless they can prove a protection-related need or a medical reason to live elsewhere. Resettlement is of equally limited value as a durable solution, since governments with major programmes, such as the United States, deem the DRC too insecure for immigration officials to visit. Therefore the major focus of the UNHCR office is the facilitation of return. Approximately 32,000 Angolans were predicted to return home in 2004. The repatriation plans for 69,000 Sudanese refugees have been postponed until the situation in Sudan is stabilised.

Challenges of providing assistance and protection to the displaced

Providing assistance and protection to civilians in the DRC is a major challenge for both the government and humanitarian actors. The biggest constraints include the volatile security situation in the east, poor infrastructure, non-existent communications, and lack of resources. In the west, donors' lack of interest in funding non-humanitarian work restricts the ability of agencies to intervene. UNOCHA estimates that of the 1.4 million IDPs in North and South Kivu, Miniema, and northern Katanga provinces, about one million are accessible to humanitarian agencies. Of those, 615,000, or 45 per cent of the total number of IDPs, receive some form of assistance.[46] In the past year, UNOCHA has signed numerous agreements with the community-based militias known as Mayi Mayi to provide free passage through 'humanitarian corridors' in areas that they control. MONUC also plays an important role, facilitating relief delivery through negotiations and escorts. Sometimes, where services do exist, people are reluctant to leave their forest refuge to claim them, because they have no clothes to wear.

Another challenge is to prioritise expenditure of funds in the face of such a large, complex crisis. As one donor noted, *'You're forced to choose between one vulnerable group and another vulnerable group'*. However, many acknowledged that IDPs and their communities of refuge often face special risks. An influx of IDPs can be *'the last fatal shock'* for poor villages.[47] Given the fluid nature of displacement, it is no simple matter to assess who qualifies for targeted assistance. In the absence of any agreed criteria, agencies are forced to apply their own, inconsistent, standards. WFP, for example, generally discontinues support for displaced populations after six months. UNICEF, on the other hand, provides non-food items and shelter for a (renewable) period of three months.[48]

Some displaced people, most of whom have been uprooted many times, live in squalid, informal settlements. One such settlement, known as Camp Areps, in Sake, North Kivu, is home to about 80 households, mainly female-headed. A 70-year-old resident described her situation to Oxfam:

> *In 1999 I fled with my children from Masisi to the forest, where we slept most nights to keep ourselves safe. In 2002 my daughter and I came to Sake. After several months we went back to see if the situation had changed. The Mayi Mayi were still fighting, so we had to return. We live like pigs here – no mattresses, no clothes. I earn 20 Congolese Francs twice a week [approximately US$.04], carrying produce to the local market. My daughter sometimes helps to farm other people's fields.*

Despite the insecurity in which they live, this woman and her family have received no assistance for nearly two years. Camp Arep's very existence – a mere 40-minute drive from Goma – serves as a vivid reminder of the vast challenges facing relief operations in the DRC.

The EU in the DRC

As described in greater detail earlier, the EU resumed formal development co-operation with the DRC in 2003. The EU is active in a wide range of sectors, from infrastructure to health, food security, policing, and justice. In addition, the EU played a prominent role in conflict reduction through its deployment of Operation Artemis in Ituri district in mid-2003.

Co-operation for Migration Management

Despite the large numbers of Congolese refugees and asylum seekers in Europe, the DRC has not been the focus of specific grants through the migration co-operation budget.[49] The current Country Strategy Paper makes only a brief mention of migration – recommending that the dynamic between migration and development be further explored. The role of remittances, assistance for the sustainable return of Congolese from Europe, and the consequences of 'brain drain' are included as possible issues to examine.[50]

The recent 'de-concentration' of Commission staff to the delegation in Kinshasa provides an enhanced opportunity to integrate immigration and asylum measures into the country strategy with meaningful input from civil society.

Oxfam's work in the DRC

The Democratic Republic of the Congo war has resulted in one of the world's worst humanitarian crises, with more than two million displaced people scattered throughout the country. An estimated 2.5 million people have died as a result of the war, many of them through preventable diseases. The crumbling state infrastructure in the health sector, as in other sectors, has been completely unable to cope. Oxfam GB's programme aims to enhance policy changes at national, regional, and international levels to maximise its impact on suffering in the DRC, especially in relation to displaced and vulnerable populations. This is intended to be a key focus of the programme in the DRC.

Oxfam GB has been present in the DRC for more than 40 years. Its programmes have aimed to meet the public-health needs of vulnerable people, focusing on education, water, sanitation, and hygiene. Oxfam is one of the few NGOs that maintained a presence in both government-controlled and rebel-held territories throughout the duration of the recent war. We currently have programmes managed by two key centres in Goma and in Kinshasa; the latter is the country management centre.

The Goma office currently supports and co-ordinates programmes in the Masisi and Beni territories of North Kivu and in Ituri. In addition, Oxfam GB continues to support and monitor an integrated water, sanitation, and malaria-control pilot project in Yakusu (Province Orientale), for which it transferred responsibility to the Health Zone Authorities in April 2003. Oxfam GB is a lead agency for water and sanitation in the east. The focus of the programme in the western part of the country will be education, and projects are scheduled to start in Kinshasa and in Mbandaka (Province Orientale) in early 2005. In 2005, Oxfam GB intends to strengthen the mainstreaming of gender-related issues, and (where feasible) the integration of malaria prevention in its programmes. The programme in the east provides important links to wider issues of protection and advocacy, in relation to campaigns on war economies, conflict management, and humanitarian crises.

Oxfam GB launched a programme to support internally displaced people in the Beni territory of North Kivu in September 2003. It focuses on emergency sanitation and hygiene promotion for internally displaced persons coming from Ituri, but also for the local population through the local NGO PPSSP, which has a good record of implementing public-health promotion activities. As an integral part of the programme, Oxfam is also working with partners to improve co-ordination in Beni and is investigating the needs of the IDP population for protection.

In Ituri, where the situation is one of the most complex and unpredictable, Oxfam GB initiated its programme in September 1999 with water, sanitation, and hygiene-promotion activities. In May 2003, following a new deterioration of the security and humanitarian situation, Oxfam launched an emergency public-health programme in Bunia and surroundings to assist internally displaced persons. In addition, Oxfam's lobbying and advocacy work arguably made a significant contribution to the stabilisation of the situation in Ituri. With restoration of peace in the Ituri area, the programme is projected in 2005 to expand support in the same fields to returnees and to local populations affected by the conflict in other locations in Ituri. ECHO, Oxfam GB, and UNICEF fund the programme.

The research consultant visited Kinshasa, Goma, and Bunia. Key informants included staff from the following institutions: Oxfam GB, MONUC, UNICEF, UN Office of the High Commissioner for Human Rights, MSF–Holland, UNOCHA, UNDP, Human Rights Watch, NRC, ICRC, ECHO, the EC Delegation, Justice Plus, Agro Action Allemande, DFID, RCN Justice et Démocratie, the Belgian Embassy, and La Voix des Sans-Voix. War-affected civilians in Camp Aero (Bunia), Camp Areps (outside Goma), and Kinshasa also contributed their stories and opinions to this report.

Notes

Glossary

1 UNHCR, Standing Committee (30th meeting), 'Protracted refugee situations' (doc. EC/54//SC/CRP.14), 10 June 2004.

Introduction

1 UNHCR Briefing Notes, 'Chad: Extreme concerns on Chad's capacity to sustain further influx from Darfur', 21 December 2004.

2 Antonio Vitorino, Commissioner responsible for Justice and Home Affairs, 'The Future of the European Union Agenda on Asylum, Migration and Borders', Conference of the European Policy Center and King Baudouin Foundation, Brussels, 4 October 2004.

3 'The Hague Programme: Strengthening Freedom, Security and Justice in the European Union', paragraph 1.6.1, Brussels European Council, 4-5 November 2004, p.13.

4 Statement by Erica Feller at the 55th session of the Executive Committee of the High Commissioner's programme, October 2004.

Chapter 1

* Source of data relating to map on p.7: Table of refugees and asylum seekers worldwide (as of December 2003) by host country, US Committee for Refugees: *World Refugee Survey*, 2004.

1 UNHCR estimates that there are 9.7 million refugees under its concern, in addition to some four million Palestinian refugees who fall under the remit of UNWRA ('Refugees by Numbers 2004', UNHCR, www.unhcr.ch).

2 The main countries of origin of refugees during 2003 were Afghanistan (2.51 million refugees), Sudan (508,200), Burundi (574,700), Democratic Republic of Congo (424,900), Somalia (432,200), Iraq (422,100), Vietnam (373,700), Liberia (275,600), and Angola (428,400). In addition, there were an estimated 428,800 Palestinian refugees.

3 UNHCR, '2003 Global Refugee Trends', Geneva: UNHCR, 15 June 2004, p. 2. NB: this excludes some four million Palestinian refugees who are covered by the mandate of UNWRA rather than UNHCR.

4 UNHCR, 'Developing countries host most refugees, according to new statistical yearbook from UNHCR', UNHCR press release, 8 November 2002.

5 UNHCR, *Statistical Yearbook 2004: Trends in Displacement, Protection and Solutions*, July 2004: 16.

6 With 4 million in Sudan alone, 3 million in the DRC, and 1.2 million in Uganda. In addition, 2.9 million people were internally displaced in Colombia, 1.1 million in Iraq, and 1 million in Burma (IDP Project, 'Internal Displacement: A Global Overview of Trends and Developments in 2003', www.idpproject.org).

7 USCR, 'World Refugee Survey 2004', www.refugees.org.

8 SPHERE (www.sphereproject.org) gives details of widely recognised minimum standards for disaster response. Basic standards, such as a nutritional intake of 2100kCal per person per day, are often not met.

9   For example, the Gatumba site for refugees from DRC in Burundi, which was attacked in August 2004. IDP camps in the north of Uganda are frequently attacked by the Lord's Resistance Army rebel group.

10   Human Rights Watch, 'Hidden in Plain View' (2001), www.hrw.org.

11   Core human-rights instruments include the Universal Declaration of Human Rights (1948); the International Convention on the Elimination of All Forms of Racial Discrimination (1965); the International Covenant on Civil and Political Rights (1966); the International Covenant on Economic, Social and Cultural Rights (1966); the UN Convention on the Elimination of All Forms of Discrimination Against Women (1979); the UN Convention Against Torture and Other Cruel, Inhuman or Degrading Treatment or Punishment (1984); and the UN Convention on the Rights of the Child (1989).

12   UNHCR, June 2002, *Agenda for Protection, Declaration of States Parties*.

13   ALNAP, *Humanitarian Protection: A Guidance Booklet,* March 2004.

14   UNHCR *Handbook on Voluntary Repatriation*, Genoa, 1996, pp 8-11. www.unhcr.ch

Chapter 2

*   Source of data relating to map on p.13: 'Asylum levels and trends in industrialised countries – third quarter 2004', UNHCR.

1   Presidency Conclusions, Tampere European Council, 15-16 October 1999, para. 3.

2   Human Rights Watch, World Report 2005, p.269.

3   For an in-depth discussion, see ECRE, 'Broken Promises – Forgotten Principles: An ECRE evaluation of the development of EU minimum standards for refugee protection, Tampere 1999 – Brussels 2004', June 2004 (available at www.ecre.org).

4   Tampere Conclusions, *op. cit.,* paras. 4, 13. The same document states the intention of the Union to 'work towards establishing a Common European Asylum System, based on the full and inclusive application of the Geneva Convention, thus ensuring that nobody is sent back to persecution' (para. 13).

5   Tampere Conclusions, *op. cit.,* para. 11.

6   Council of the European Union, 'Multiannual Strategic Programme', Council doc. 15420/03 of December 1, 2003, para. 36.

7   Declaration 17 (on Article 73k of the Treaty establishing the European Community), Final Act of the Treaty of Amsterdam amending the Treaty on European Union, the Treaties establishing the European Communities and certain related acts, 2 October 1997.

8   Tampere Conclusions, *op. cit.,* para. 14.

9   In an April 1999 Resolution, for example, the European Parliament emphasised that, with asylum now placed within the 'first pillar' of the EU, there was a 'need for open and detailed consultation with the UNHCR and citizens' organisations' (European Parliament's April 1999 Resolution on the Strategy Paper on the EU's Migration and Asylum Policy. Doc. A4-0143/99; Minutes of 13 April 1999).

Chapter 3

1   R. Lubbers, 'EU should share asylum responsibilities, not shift them', 5 November 2004, www.unhcr.ch.

2   See, *inter alia,* ECRE June 2004, *op. cit.*; Amnesty International, 'Threatening Refugee Protection: Amnesty International's Overall Assessment of the Tampere Asylum Agenda, June 1999–May 2004', July 2004; UK Refugee Council, 'Refugee Council Briefing on the Common European Asylum System', March 2004.

3   Tampere Conclusions, *op. cit.,* paras. 11-27.

4   Article 63, Treaty Establishing the European Community (consolidated text – see Official Journal C 325, 24 December 2002), incorporating Article 73k, Treaty of Amsterdam, *op. cit.* See also Tampere Conclusions, *op. cit.,* paras 14, 16.

5   Tampere Conclusions, *op. cit.,* Annex I, p.13.

6   ECRE June 2004, *op. cit.*, 25.

7   This is because once the first stage of the CEAS is complete, asylum legislation will be made by 'co-decision'.

8   Council of the European Union, 'Council Directive on the Right to Family Reunification', 22 September 2003 (doc. 2003/86/EC). In December 2003, following action by a coalition of NGOs, the President of the European Parliament instituted proceedings at the European Court of Justice to annul this directive. (An advisory opinion is expected in early 2005.)

9   Council of the European Union, 'Council Directive on Minimum Standards for the Qualification and Status of Third Country Nationals or Stateless Persons as Refugees or as Persons who Otherwise Need International Protection and the Content of the Protection Granted', 27 April 2004 (doc. 8043/04) ('Qualification Directive').

10 *Ibid.*, art. 9.2 (f). For in-depth discussion, see UNHCR, 'Guidelines on International Protection: Gender-related persecution within the context of Article 1(A)2 of the 1951 Convention and/or its 1967 Protocol Relating to the Status of Refugees', 7 May 2002 (doc. HCR/GIP/02/01).

11 *Ibid.*, art. 7.1 (b).

12 This issue remains unresolved, following the case of *Bankovic v Belgium and others* (European Court of Human Rights, December 2001).

13 The International Rescue Committee (2003), 'Mortality in the Democratic Republic of Congo: Results from a Nationwide Survey', www.theirc.org/drc (last checked November 2004).

14 Human Rights Watch (2003), 'Ituri: Covered in Blood', http://hrw.org/reports/2003/ituri0703/DRC0703-01.htm#P128_3579http://hrw.org/reports/2003/ituri0703/DRC0703-01.htm#P128_3579

15 UN Security Council Resolution 1484 (2003), http://daccess-ods.un.org/TMP/9212475.html (last checked November 2004).

16 United Nations Integrated Regional Information Networks (IRIN) (2003), 'DRC: EU calls Artemis operation "a big success"', www.irinnews.org/report.asp?ReportID=36655 (last checked November 2004).

17 Interview with UNDP, Bunia.

18 UN Security Council (2004), 'Third special report of the Secretary-General on the United Nations Organization Mission in the Democratic Republic of the Congo', New York: UNSC, p. 22.

19 UN Security Council (2004), 'UN SC extends DRC mission until 31 March 2005, authorizes additional 5,900 troops, police – Unanimously adopts resolution 1565', www.reliefweb.int/w/rwb.nsf/0/06ccbb66a42e0f0d49256f230008ec39?OpenDocument (last checked November 2004).

20 Kate Holt and Sarah Hughes (2004), 'Sex and death in the heart of Africa', http://news.independent.co.uk/world/africa/story.jsp?story=524557 (last checked November 2004).

21 UN Security Council (2004), 'Third Special Report on MONUC', *op. cit.*, p.8.

22 Interview with UNOCHA, Bunia.

23 Council of the European Union, 'Amended Proposal for a Council Directive on Minimum Standards on Procedures in Member States for Granting and Withdrawing Refugee Status', 30 April 2004 (doc. 8771/04).

24 ECRE *et al.*, 'Call for Withdrawal of the Asylum Procedures Directive', 22 March 2004; see also UNHCR, 'Aide Memoire: Directive on Minimum Standards on Procedures for Granting and Withdrawing Refugee Status', 18 November 2003; Amnesty International, July 2004, *op. cit.;* ECRE, June 2004, *op. cit.*

25 UNHCR News Stories, 'Lubbers warns of deteriorating standards in EU asylum directive', 24 November 2003.

26 See art. 33 of the 1951 Refugee Convention; art. 3 of the European Convention on Human Rights; art. 3 of the Convention Against Torture; art. 7 of the International Covenant on Civil and Political Rights; and arts. 18, 19, 47 of the Charter of Fundamental Rights of the European Union.

27 The Directive provides two sets of criteria for Safe Third Countries. (Arts. 27.1 27.2 apply where asylum seekers enter the EU legally, while 35a.1 and 35a.2 apply where asylum seekers enter illegally.) By defining STCs differently on the basis of an asylum seeker's method of entry to the EU, member states might, considering the potential consequences for the individual, be acting contrary to art. 31 of the 1951 Refugee Convention.

28 See also ECRE, 'ECRE's Recommendations to the Justice and Home Affairs Council on the "Safe Third Country" concept at its meeting on 22-23 January 2004', 15 January 2004 .

29 Procedures Directive, *op cit.,* art. 30.1, 30B (2).

30 *Ibid.,* art. 30.2, 30.7.

31 Council of the European Union, 'Amended Proposal for a Council Directive on Minimum Standards on Procedures in Member States for Granting and Withdrawing Refugee Status – Minimum Common List of Safe Countries of Origin', 26 May 2004 (doc. 8772/04).

32 Statewatch, 'EU divided over list of "safe countries of origin" – the list should be scrapped', 27 September 2004.

33 UNHCR, 'Sri Lanka Background Paper', *op. cit.*, p. 15.

34 ' Annual Report: Sri Lanka', http://web.amnesty.org/report2004/lka-summary-eng (last checked November 2004). Interviews with the HRC in Trincomalee, Vavuniya, and Batticaloa.

35 Article 2.1 of the Ceasefire Agreement provides that 'the parties shall in accordance with international law abstain from hostile acts against the civilian population, including such acts as torture, intimidation, abduction, extortion and harassment' (Agreement on a Ceasefire Between the Government of the Democratic Socialist Republic of Sri Lanka and the Liberation Tigers of Tamil Eelam', www.peaceinsri-lanka.com/insidepages/Agreement/agceasefire.asp, last checked November 2004).

36 UNHCR (2004), 'Background Paper on Refugees and Asylum-Seekers from Sri Lanka', www.unhcr.ch/cgibin/texis/vtx/publ/opendoc.pdf?tbl=RSDCOI&id=40d837f42&page=publ (last checked November 2004).

37 UNHCR Sri Lanka Background Paper, *op. cit.,* p. 13.

38 Human Rights Watch (2004), 'Sri Lanka: New Killings Threaten Ceasefire', http://hrw.org/english/docs/2004/07/27/slanka9153_txt.htm (last checked November 2004).

39 UNICEF, 'Recruitment and Re-recruitment after January 2002', chart provided to author.

40 UNICEF, 'Recruitment Gender Analysis', provided by email to author in October 2004.

41 Interview with SLMM, Vavuniya.

42 Interview with Forum for Human Development, Colombo.

43 Interview with Nonviolent Peace Force, Valaichchenai.

44 UNHCR, 'Handbook on Procedures and Criteria for Determining Refugee Status under the 1951 Convention and the 1967 Protocol relating to the Status of Refugees', 1992 (paras. 37-43).

45 UNHCR, 'UNHCR doubts on the readiness of Slovak asylum policy to enter the EU', April 2004.

46 Advisory Panel on Country Information, 'Report of Advisory Panel on Country Information Consultation Exercise on CIPU Country Reports October 2003', 2 March 2004; R. Ford, 'Refugees judged on flawed assessments', *The Times*, 1 May 2004; Immigration Advisory Service, 'Home Office Country Assessments: An Analysis', September 2003.

47 UK House of Lords (European Union Committee), 'Handling EU Asylum Claims: New Approaches Examined', 11th Report of Session 2003-4, 30 April 2004 (paras. 114-17).

Chapter 4

1. UNHCR's Executive Committee has frequently reaffirmed 'the fundamental importance of the observance of the principle of *non-refoulement* – both at the border and within the territory of a State – of persons who may be subjected to persecution if returned to their country of origin, irrespective of whether or not they have been formally recognised as refugees' (UNHCR EXCOM Conclusions No.6, XXVIII, 1977, para. c).

2. UNHCR, *Agenda for Protection*, 3rd edition, p.12.

3. Council of the European Union, 'Communication on a Common Policy on Illegal Immigration, European Commission', COM (2001) 672 Final, 15 November 2001 (para. 3.2).

4. As a UK judge has commented, 'Although under the Convention subscribing States must give sanctuary to any refugee who seeks asylum (subject only to removal to a safe third country), they are by no means bound to facilitate his arrival. Rather they strive increasingly to prevent it. The combined effect of visa requirements and carrier's liability has made it well nigh impossible for refugees to travel to countries of refuge without false documents' (Lord Justice Simon Brown, Judgement in *Uxbridge Magistrates Court and Another ex parte Adimi,* UK Court of Appeal, 29 July 1999, Case Ref. CO-1167-99).

5. ECRE, June 2004, *op. cit.,* p. 17.

6. United for Intercultural Action, 'List of 5017 Documented Refugee Deaths through Fortress Europe', Information Leaflet No. 24, 16 June 2004.

7. The access dilemma is discussed in detail in ECRE and US Committee for Refugees, 'Responding to the Asylum and Access Challenge: An Agenda for Comprehensive Engagement in Protracted Refugee Situations', April 2003.

8. Council Regulation (EC) No. 2007/2004, establishing a European Agency for the Management of Operational Cooperation at the External Borders of the Member States of the European Union, 26 October 2004 (published in the Official Journal of the EC, 25 November 2004 – L 349/1).

9. In its opinion on a draft version of this Regulation, the European Economic and Social Committee had stressed that the right of asylum, the principle of non-refoulement, and international conventions on human rights must be respected, and that training for border guards, to be provided by the Agency, must emphasise this (Official Journal of the European Union, C 108, 30 April 2004). However, the Council appears to have ignored this recommendation, as the adopted regulation makes no specific reference to the right of asylum or the principle of non-refoulement.

10. International Law Commission, *Draft Articles on Responsibility of States for Internationally Wrongful Acts*, articles 6 and 7, adopted ILC 53rd session, 2001.

11. See I. Brownlie, *System of Law of Nations: State Responsibility, Part I,* 1983, Clarendon Press, Oxford; G. Goodwin-Gill, *The Refugee in International Law,* 2nd ed. 1996, Clarendon Press, Oxford.

12. UNHCR Executive Committee (Standing Committee), 'Interception of Asylum-Seekers and Refugees: The International Framework and Recommendations for a Comprehensive Approach' (doc. EC/50/SC/CRP.17), 9 June 2000.

13. Council Regulation (EC) No. 377/2004 on the creation of an immigration liaison officers network, 19 February 2004 (published in Official Journal of the European Union, L 64/1, 2 March 2004).

14. Of course, low acceptance rates for a certain group do not obviate the need for each and every asylum claim to be examined on its merits; how else can those members of this group who *are* in need of protection be identified?

15. House of Lords, Opinions of the Lords of Appeal for Judgement in the cause *Regina (ex parte European Roma Rights Centre and others) appellant Vs the Immigration Officer at Prague Airport, and another (respondents)* (Case No. [2004] UKHL55, 9 December 2004); see *inter alia* paras. 26, 68, 71, 104.

16 UNHCR Executive Committee (Standing Committee), 'Interception of Asylum-Seekers and Refugees: The International Framework and Recommendations for a Comprehensive Approach' (doc. EC/50/SC/CRP.17), 9 June 2000, para. 23.

17 For further details on these initiatives, see British Refugee Council, 'Barriers to Protection', forthcoming 2005.

18 UNHCR press release, 'UNHCR criticises handling of Cap Anamur asylum claims', 23 July 2004.

19 UNHCR press release, 'UNHCR deeply concerned over returns from Italy', 4 October 2004; Amnesty International, 'Italy: human rights of refugees violated', 5 October 2004; S. Gabbio, 'Refugees: fate of hundreds unknown', *International Press Service*, 5 October 2004.

20 In the early 1990s, the US Coast Guard regularly interdicted Haitian asylum seekers on the high seas. The US authorities repatriated these Haitians, without offering the possibility of screening to those who might qualify as refugees (see, *inter alia*, G. Goodwin-Gill, 1996, *op. cit.*). In a similar vein, in August 2001 the Australian government prevented the *MV Tampa*, a Norwegian freighter, from disembarking more than 400 asylum-seekers who had been rescued from an overloaded vessel. Although many of those on board the *Tampa* were in need of urgent medical attention, the ship was refused entry to Australia, and the asylum seekers were transferred to another ship, to be expelled from Australian territorial waters. Australia then negotiated agreements with Nauru to take the intercepted asylum seekers, who were to be confined in camps run by the International Organisation for Migration. See Human Rights Watch, 'By Invitation Only: Australian Asylum Policy', 10 December 2002 (HRW Index No. C1410).

21 Council of the European Union, 'Council Directive Supplementing the Provisions of Article 26 of the Convention implementing the Schengen Agreement of 14 June 1985' (2001/51/EC) 28 June 2001 (arts. 4(2), 3).

22 See Amnesty International, 'Eritrea: Country Report on Human Rights Practices 2003', US Department of State, 25 February 2004: para.1d; Amnesty International, 'You have no right to ask: Government resists scrutiny on human rights', 19 May 2004 (AI Index: AFR 64/003/2004): 30ff.

23 Belgian Presidency of the EU, 'Presidency Contribution to the European Conference on Migration, Panel No 3 Partnership with Countries of Origin – Experience of the Council of the European Union's High Level Working Group on Asylum and Migration', 3 October 2001, SN 4107/1/02.

24 Presidency Conclusions, Seville European Council, 21-22 June 2002, paras. 33-36.

25 Die Bundesregierung, 'Results of the Seville European Council', 25 July 2002 (www.bundesregierung.de/en/News-by-subject/Europe-,11057/EU-summits.htm). See also F. Pastore, 'Cooperation with Sending and Transit Countries: Beyond Sticks and Carrots', paper presented at the (Dutch) Presidency Conference on Future European Union Co-operation on Asylum, Migration and Frontiers, Amsterdam, 31 August–3 September 2004 (www.migrationpolicy.org/events/pastore_083104.pdf).

26 Serbia and Montenegro was later added to this list, because the name of the country changed and it was no longer considered FY Yugoslavia.

27 Even though no association agreement had yet been concluded with Libya. See Council of the EU, 2469th Council Meeting, Justice and Home Affairs, Brussels, 28-29 November 2002: 14817/02 (Presse 375), p.13. For details on progress of EU co-operation with each of these countries, see Commission of the European Communities, 'Commission Staff Working Paper: Intensified Cooperation on the Management of Migration Flows with Third Countries' (SEC 2003 (815)), 9 July 2003 (www.statewatch.org/news/2003/jul/comsec11450en03.pdf).

28 Presidency Conclusions, Seville European Council, 21-22 June 2002, para. 34.

29 Council of the European Union, 'Road Map for the Follow Up to the Conclusions of the European Council in Seville – Asylum, Immigration and Border Control', 20 November 2002 (doc. 10525/3/02/REV 3); see also 2469th Council Meeting, Justice and Home Affairs, *op. cit.*, p.6.

30 Treaty Establishing a Constitution for Europe, Article III 267(3).

31 ECRE, June 2003, *op. cit.*; Amnesty International, July 2004, *op. cit.*

32 The European Commission stated, in a 2001 Communication, that the negotiation of readmission agreements should be preceded by an evaluation of the political and human-rights situation in the relevant third country (Commission of the European Communities, 'Communication on a Common Policy on Illegal Immigration', COM (2001), 672 final, p. 25).

33 S. Spiteri, 'Prompt lifting of Chinese arms embargo improbable, says Prodi', *EU Observer*, 14 April 2004.

34 A readmission clause was included in the EU's Association Agreement with Syria, adopted 9 December 2003. For more details, see Amnesty International, 'A Critical Analysis of EU Asylum Policy: the Fall from Tampere', March 2004, p.10; and ECRE, June 2004, *op. cit.*, p. 23.

35 Interview with Director, Forum for Human Development, Colombo.

36 Interview with Deputy High Commissioner, British High Commission, Colombo.

37 Interview with returned asylum seeker, Kilinochchi.

38 The ENP was first outlined in the Commission Communication, 'Wider Europe – Neighbourhood: A new framework for relations with our Eastern and Southern Neighbours', 11 March 2003, COM (2003) 104 final. In October 2003 the European Council welcomed this initiative and requested the Commission and Council of Ministers to take it forward. The agreements were approved on 9 December 2004 (A. Beatty, 'Brussels approves "neighbourhood" deals', *EU Observer,* 9 December 2004).

39 The Southern Caucasus has been identified as an important region within the context of the 2003 European Security Strategy (European Commission Press Release, 'Beyond Enlargement: Commission Shifts European Neighbourhood Policy into Higher Gear', doc. IP/04/632, 12 May 2004).

40 A. Beatty, 9 December 2004, *op. cit.*; see also A. Beatty, 'Landmark neighbourhood strategy to be approved', *EU Observer*, 11 May 2004.

41 Commission Communication, 'European Neighbourhood Policy: Strategy Paper', COM (2004) 373 final, 12 May 2004. See also 'Beyond Enlargement: Commission Shifts European Neighbourhood Policy into Higher Gear', *op. cit.*

42 Morocco, Russia, Algeria, Ukraine, Belarus, and Moldova are the countries mentioned (Commission Communication, 'Wider Europe – Neighbourhood: A New Framework for Relations with our Eastern and Southern Neighbours', *op. cit.*, p. 11).

43 Communication, 'European Neighbourhood Policy: Strategy Paper', *op. cit.*, pp. 16-17, 21, 23.

44 For details of protection gaps in prospective ENP countries, see, *inter alia,* Human Rights Watch, 'Overview of Human Rights Developments 2002: Ukraine', 1 January 2003. For details of ratifications of 1951 Refugee Convention, see www.unhcr.ch.

45 See, for example, Communication, 'Wider Europe – Neighbourhood', *op. cit.*; also Communication 'European Neighbourhood Policy: Strategy Paper', *op. cit.*

46 See, *inter alia*, Human Rights Watch, 'Libya blocks visit by rights group: torture, political trials, treatment of migrants remain major concerns', 7 December 2004; Human Rights Watch, 'Overview of Human Rights Developments 2003: Belarus', 1 January 2004.

47 See Commission of the European Communities, 'Call for proposals 2003: Budget Line "Co-operation with Third Countries in the area of migration"'; 'Regulation (EC) No. 491/2004 of the European Parliament and of the Council Establishing a Programme for Financial and Technical Assistance to Third Countries in the Areas of Migration and Asylum (AENEAS)', 10 March 2004 (published in Official Journal of EC, L 80/1, 18 March 2004).

48 UNHCR, 'No role in North Africa's reception centres, says UNHCR', 1 October 2004.

Chapter 5

* Source of data relating to map on p.47: 'Easy guide on refugee resettlement programs 2003/2004', UNHCR, February 2004.

1 Committee on Civil Liberties, Justice and Home Affairs, Report on Asylum Procedure and Protection in Regions of Origin (2004/2121(INI)), 29 November 2004.

2   ECRE and US Committee for Refugees, April 2003, *op. cit.,* 15.

3   UNHCR, 'New Directions for Resettlement Policy and Practice', Standing Committee 21st Meeting (doc. EC/51/SC/INF.2), 14 June 2001, para. 24.

4   F. Roscam-Abbing, 'Managed arrival of persons in need of international protection as part of the Tampere II EU Asylum Agenda', Records of the International Seminar: *'Towards More Orderly and Managed Entry in the EU of Persons in Need of International Protection'*, Rome, 13-14 October 2003, p. 67.

5   H. Crawley, 'The UK, the EU and Forced Migration', Commissioned Paper for Refugee Studies Centre, Research Consultancy on Developing DFID's Approach to Refugees, Asylum Seekers and Internally Displaced People, December 2004, p. 34 (unpublished, draft cited with author's permission).

6   *Ibid.*, p. 15.

7   *Ibid.*, p. 15. See also US Committee for Refugees, 'Sea Change: Australia's New Approach to Asylum Seekers', February 2002: pp. 26, 41 (www.refugees.org).

8   For further details on global resettlement practices, see Migration Policy Institute, 'Study on the Feasibility of Setting Up Resettlement Schemes in EU Member States or at EU level, Against the Background of the Common European Asylum System and the Goal of a Common Asylum Procedure', study carried out on behalf of the European Commission, May 2004. See also ECRE and US Committee for Refugees, April 2003, *op. cit.*

9   Presidency Conclusions, Thessaloniki European Council, 19-20 June 2003, para. 26; see also Commission of the European Communities, 'Towards More Accessible, Equitable and Managed Asylum Systems', COM (2003) 315 final, 3 June 2003.

10 Commission of the European Communities, 'On the Managed Entry in the EU of Persons in Need of International Protection and the Enhancement of the Protection Capacities of the Regions of Origin', COM (2004) 410 final, 7 June 2004: para. 22.

11 See ECRE and US Committee for Refugees, April 2003, *op. cit.,* p.19.

12 Commission of the European Communities, June 2004, *op. cit.,* para. 27.

13 *Ibid.,* para. 16.

14 See ECRE and US Committee for Refugees, April 2003, *op. cit.*

15 Figures in this section were provided by UNHCR Tanzania.

16 Interview with Ministry of Home Affairs, Dar es Salaam. Certain countries, notably in Scandinavia, do target extremely vulnerable individuals, such as people with severe medical or psychological problems, in their resettlement programmes.

17 Human Rights Watch (2002), 'The War Within the War: Sexual Violence Against Women and Girls in Eastern Congo', www.hrw.org/reports/2002/drc/ (last checked November 2004).

18 MSF-Holland (2004), 'I Have No Joy, No Peace of Mind: Medical, Psychosocial, and Socio-Economic Consequences of Sexual Violence in Eastern DRC'.

19 Interview conducted by Jane Beesley, Oxfam GB.

20 UNHCR (2003), 'UNHCR Country Operations Plan 2004 – United Republic of Tanzania', www.unhcr.ch/cgi-bin/texis/vtx/country?iso=tza (last checked November 2004).

21 For details, see UNHCR, 'UNHCR Calls for Government Rethink on Zimbabwe Visas', 20 January 2003; (UK) Refugee Council, 'British Government Imposes Visa Restrictions on Zimbabwean Nationals', 8 November 2002.

22 There is also some evidence that the remaining member states (Greece, Finland, and Sweden), as well as Norway, have facilitated access on some specific occasions. For full details see Danish Centre for Human Rights, 'Study on the Feasibility of Processing Asylum Claims outside the EU against the Background of the Common European Asylum System and the Goal of a Common Asylum Procedure', study carried out on behalf of the European Commission, March 2003.

23 Commission of the European Communities, 'On the Common Asylum Policy and the Agenda for Protection', COM (2003) 152 final, 26 March 2003, p.9.

24 Danish Centre for Human Rights, March 2003, *op. cit.,* 250.

25 See, for example, presentations by member states' representatives at the October 2003 Rome Conference, *op. cit.,* pp. 71-84.

26 Commission of the European Communities, June 2004, *op. cit.,* para. 34.

27 Interview with IOM, Colombo.

28 All figures in this section were provided as estimates by the Embassy of Switzerland in Colombo.

29 Migration Policy Institute, May 2004, *op. cit.,* p. 172.

30 Commission of the European Communities, June 2003, *op. cit.,* p. 15.

31 Danish Centre for Human Rights, March 2003, *op. cit.,* p. 230.

Chapter 6

1 Cited in A. Travis, 'EU revives Blunkett's asylum camp plan', *Guardian,* 20 September 2004.

2 European Parliament, 'European Parliament Resolution on Asylum-Seekers and Migrants – Action Plans for Countries of Origin or Transit. High Level Working Group', 30 March 2000 (published in the Official Journal of the EC, C 378/75, 29 December 2000, paras. 13, 16).

3 Tony Blair, 'New International Approaches to Asylum Processing and Protection', correspondence from Tony Blair, Prime Minister of the United Kingdom, to H.E. Costas Simitis, Prime Minister of Greece and President of the European Council, 10 March 2003.

4 The 1950 European Convention on Human Rights (ECHR) provides that 'no one shall be subject to torture or to inhuman or degrading treatment or punishment' (art. 3). All EU member states are party to the ECHR, and are thus legally obliged 'to secure to everyone within their jurisdiction' the rights and freedoms defined in the Convention (art. 1).

5 See Oxfam GB, 'Written Evidence to the House of Lords Select Committee on the EU, Sub-committee F', September 2003.

6 For details, see Human Rights Watch, 'An Unjust "Vision" for Europe's Refugees: Human Rights Watch Commentary on the UK's "New Vision" Proposal for the Establishment of Refugee Processing Centres Abroad', 17 June 2003.

7 See, *inter alia,* Amnesty International, 'Unlawful and Unworkable: Amnesty International's Views on Proposals for Extra-territorial Processing of Asylum Claims' (doc. 10R61/004/2003), 18 June 2003; UK Refugee Council, 'Unsafe Havens, Unworkable Solutions', May 2003.

8 European Parliament (Committee on Civil Liberties, Justice and Home Affairs), 'Report on Asylum Procedures and Protection in Regions of Origin' (doc. 2004/2121 (INI)), 29 November 2004, para. 12.

9 Commission of the European Communities, June 2003, *op. cit.*

10 UNHCR, *Refugees by Numbers*, Geneva, 2003.

11 Commission of the European Communities, June 2004, *op. cit.,* para. 41.

12 Thessaloniki Council, *op. cit.,* paras. 26-27.

13 Commission of the European Communities, June 2004, *op. cit.*

14 UNHCR, Statement by Ms Erika Feller, Director, Department of International Protection, at the Fifty-fourth session of the Executive Committee of the High Commissioner's programme, October 2003.

15 UNHCR, Statement by Ms Erika Feller, Director, Department of International Protection, at the Fifty-fifth session of the Executive Committee of the High Commissioner's programme, October 2004.

16 Commission of the European Communities, June 2004, *op. cit.*

17 Statistics provided to author by UNHCR Field Office, Kigoma.

18   *Ibid.*

19   UNHCR–Tanzania (2004) 'Lugufu Camp Profile', provided to author by email.

20   Interview with UNHCR, Kigoma.

21   Interview with Ministry of Home Affairs, Kigoma.

22   Interview with UNHCR, Kigoma.

23   The SPHERE Project (2004), *The SPHERE Handbook*, Oxford: Oxfam GB.

24   WFP Tanzania (2004), 'The Coping Strategies Index (CSI) Baseline Survey: World Food Programme (WFP) Assisted Refugees in Western Tanzania', www.refugees.org/world/countryindex/tanzania.cfm (last checked November 2004).

25   UNHCR (2004), 'Global Report 2003: United Republic of Tanzania'.

26   Interview with UNHCR, Kigoma.

27   Interview with World Vision Sexual and Gender-Based Violence Officer (Acting), Lugufu I.

28   Such as that carried out by UNHCR in East Africa, financed under EU Budget Line B7-667; see Chapter 4.

29   For details of this project, see UNHCR, 'Convention Plus: The Strengthening Protection Capacity (SPC) Project', 17 November 2004; UNHCR, 'Framework for Identifying Gaps in Protection Capacity', 25 November 2004. For details of EU funding mechanism B7-667, see Commission of the European Communities, 'B7-667 – Call for Proposals 2003 – Proposals Selected and Reserve List'.

30   Commission of the European Communities, June 2004, *op. cit.,* para. 50.

31   M. Smith, 'Warehousing refugees: a denial of rights, a waste of humanity', in US Committee for Refugees, *World Refugee Survey 2004: Warehousing Issue*, p. 44; see also J. Crisp, 'Mind the Gap: UNHCR, Humanitarian Assistance and the Development Process', *New Issues in Refugee Research,* Working Paper No. 43, May 2001.

32   One of the stated objectives for the UK's 'New Vision' plan was to 'reduce the incentive for the minority [of refugees in regions of origin] who do move on to Europe to do so'(Tony Blair letter, 10 March 2003, *op. cit.*).

33   In the June 2003 Communication, for example, the Commission specifies that the overall aim of the 'new approach' is to enable persons in need of international protection to access this protection 'as soon as possible and as closely as possible to their needs, *and therewith reducing felt needs and pressures to seek international protection elsewhere*' (Commission of the European Communities, June 2003, *op. cit*:, p. 13 (emphasis added)).

34   The Dutch government has been forthright regarding its own motivations for seeking increased EU activity in regions of origin: 'to effect a gradual separation between the flows of refugees and economic migrants in the asylum procedure, which are now mixed, and to relieve the pressure on this procedure. [..] the government also hopes that making international agreements about protection in the region will have a favourable impact on the implementation of repatriation policy' ('Letter on Protection in the Region', Joint Letter from Dutch Ministries of Foreign Affairs, Immigration and Integration, and Development Co-operation, to the President of the House of Representatives of the States General (doc. DPV/AM-270/03), 28 May 2003: p. 1).

35   Commission of the European Communities, June 2004, *op. cit.,* paras. 13, 15.

36   Oxfam International (2003), *Beyond the Headlines. An agenda for action to protect civilians in neglected conflicts,* p.32.

37   Joint Letter from Dutch Ministries, 28 May 2003, *op. cit.*, p. 15.

38   M. Beunderman, 'EU asylum centres in north Africa proposed', *EU Observer*, 20 July 2004.

39   In August 2004, Italian officials discussed this idea with Col. Ghadaffy. (See E. Jozsef, 'A Tripoli, Berluscoini croit enrayer l'immigration', *Libération*, 26 August 2004; P. Popham, 'Italy asks Gaddaffi to halt tide of migrants', *Independent,* 24 August 2004.)

40   Brussels European Council, 4-5 November 2004, *op. cit.*, 13 (emphasis added).

41   See, for example, the comments of the UK House of Lords European Union Committee, 30 April 2004, *op. cit.*, paras. 132, 135, 140-143.

Chapter 7

1   Tampere European Council, 15-16 October 1999, *op. cit.*, para. 11.

2   UNHCR, *Agenda for Protection*, 3rd edition, October 2003, Geneva.

3   Treaty of Amsterdam, *op. cit.*, art. 10; art. 11 (Title V) of the Treaty on European Union (consolidated text).

4   1951 Convention relating to the Status of Refugees, art. 1(A)2.

5   Treaty of Amsterdam, *op. cit.*, art. 1.8 (a); Treaty on European Union (consolidated text): art. 6.

6   Brussels European Council, 4-5 November 2004, *op. cit.*, p.11.

7   Commission of the European Communities, 'On the Role of the European Union in Promoting Human Rights and Democratisation in Third Countries', 8 May 2001, COM (2001) 252 final.

8   A. Hammerstad, 'Making or Breaking the Conflict Cycle: The Relationship between Conflict, Underdevelopment and Forced Migration', submitted to the Refugee Studies Centre, Oxford University, and DFID, August 2004 (unpublished, cited with author's permission); S. Castles, H. Crawley, S Loughna, *States of Conflict: Causes and Patterns of Forced Migration to the EU and Policy Responses*, 2003, Institute for Public Policy Research, London.

9   Castles *et al.*, 2003, *op. cit.*

10   Oxfam GB, 2003, *op. cit.*, p.18.

11   See Charter of the United Nations, Chapter I (art. 1), Chapter VII (arts. 39-42).

12   United Nations Press Release, 'Secretary General names High Level Panel to study global security threats, and recommend necessary changes' (doc. SG/A/857), 4 November 2003.

13   At present, conflict prevention is more of an *implicit* goal of CFSP: the Treaty on European Union states the objective of 'preserving peace and strengthening international security' (art. 11.3 TEU).

14   These include a 2001 Communication on Conflict Prevention (11 April 2001, COM (2001), 211 final); a 2003 Communication on the EU–Africa Dialogue (23 June 2003, COM (2003), 316 final); a 2003 Communication on Governance and Development (20 October 2003, COM (2003) 615 final), and also the 2003 European Security Strategy, 'A Secure Europe in a Better World' (prepared by Javier Solana, adopted at the Brussels European Council, 12 December 2003).

15   For details, see www.europa.eu.int/comm/external_relations/cpcm/mission/index.htm

16   See http://ue.eu.int/cms3_fo/showPage.asp?id=584&lang=EN&mode=g

17   The Regulation establishing the Rapid Reaction Mechanism was adopted by the General Affairs Council on 26 February 2001. See also Commission of the European Communities, 'Communication on Financial Perspectives 2007–2013', 14 July 2004, COM (2004) 487 final, p. 23.

18   SaferWorld and International Alert, 'Strengthening Global Security through Addressing the Root Causes of Conflict: Priorities for the Irish and Dutch Presidencies in 2004', February 2004: pp. 44-9.

19   Castles *et al.*, *op. cit.*, p. 28; see also A. Hammerstad, August 2004, *op. cit.*

20   See, *inter alia*, Commission of the European Communities, 'Integrating Migration Issues in the European Union's Relations with Third Countries', 3 December 2002, COM (2002) 703 final.

21   Title II of the Cotonou Agreement provides that ACP States commit themselves to 'accept the return of and the readmission of any of its nationals who are illegally present on the territory of a member state of the European Union, at that member state's request and without further formalities' (art. 13.5(c)i). Full text available at www.europa.eu.int/comm/development/body/cotonou/agreement_en.htm

22   Castles *et al.*, *op. cit.*, p. 51.

23 Commission of the European Communities, 'ECHO Aid Strategy 2004', 18 December 2003, pp. 3, 8.

24 On the basis of this approach, ECHO committed itself to respond to a variety of 'forgotten crises' throughout 2004, including those in Western Sahara, Haiti, Nepal, Somalia, and Myanmar / Burma (*ibid.,* p. 4).

25 UN Security Council (2001), 'Addendum to the Report of the Panel of Experts on the Illegal Exploitation of Natural Resources and Other Forms of Wealth of DR Congo'.

26 Odhiambo Anacleti (2004), 'Prevailing Problems and Prospects for the Great Lakes Region: A Contribution to the National Civil Society Meeting to Prepare a National Input for Regional Meeting or Regional Civil Society Meeting on the Great Lakes Region, August 30-31 2004', p.7.

27 In this report, the term 'Banyamulenge' will be used in a broad sense to refer to Congolese of Tutsi origin. 'Banyamulenge' literally refers to 'people from the Mulenge area'; it was originally coined by the Congolese government to distinguish immigrants from Rwanda who arrived after 1959 from those who came earlier (ActionAid, 1997, 'Understanding the Great Lakes Crisis').

28 United Nations Development Programme (2004), 'UNDP Newsletter on DDR in the Democratic Republic of the Congo'.

29 International Crisis Group (2004), 'Africa Briefing: Pulling Back from the Brink in the Congo'.

30 EC and the DRC (2003) 'Strategie de Cooperation et Programme Indicatif 2003–2007'.

31 *Ibid.*, p. 28.

32 Interview with the DRC Desk Officer, Brussels.

33 According to the DRC Desk Officer in Brussels, development is seen as a tool for increasing civilian security: 'All of our projects, especially the LRRD (Linking Relief, Rehabilitation and Development) projects in the East, contribute to resolution of conflict in the DRC.'

34 The DRC occupies first place on ECHO's vulnerability index (GINA: Global Index for Humanitarian Needs Assessment), which considers criteria such as child-mortality rates and the UNDP Human Development Ranking (European Commission Humanitarian Aid Office, 2003, 'Humanitarian Aid to Vulnerable Population Groups in the Democratic Republic of Congo (DRC), Global Plan 2004'). Indeed, the DRC is thought to have the highest mortality rates in the world, with average infant-mortality rates for the whole of Eastern Congo at 3 /10,000 /day (50 per cent above the emergency threshold). *Ibid.,* p.7.

35 Interview with ECHO Representative, Kinshasa.

36 ECHO (2004).

37 International Criminal Court (2004), press release, 'The Office of the Prosecutor of the International Criminal Court opens its first investigation.

38 The most visible regional initiative is the World Bank's Multi-Country Demobilization and Reintegration Program, which disburses funds for numerous DDR projects in central Africa.

39 For a detailed discussion, see Amnesty International, IANSA, and Oxfam GB (The Control Arms Campaign), *Guns or Growth? Assessing the Impact of Arms Sales on Sustainable Development,* published in association with Ploughshares and Saferworld, June 2004, p. 2.

40 *Ibid.*, p. 4.

41 Two obvious examples are Pakistan and Tanzania (*ibid.,* p. 3).

42 The Control Arms Campaign, June 2004, *op. cit.,* p. 4.

43 *Ibid.,* p. 14.

44 UN Programme of Action to Prevent, Combat and Eradicate the Illicit Trade in Small Arms and Light Weapons in all its Aspects, 2001, Section 2, para. 11.

45 Saferworld, 'Taking Control: The Case for a More Effective European Union Code of Conduct on Arms Exports – a report by European Union non-governmental organisations', September 2004; see also A. Beatty, 'Loopholes in arms controls exposed', *EU Observer*, 30 September 2004.

46   See Amnesty International, IANSA, and Oxfam GB (The Control Arms Campaign), June 2004, *op. cit*.

47   See Common Position of 16 April 1999 (published in Official Journal L 103, 20 April 1999).

48   Council of the European Union, press release, 2609th Council Meeting, General Affairs and External Relations (External Relations), Luxembourg, 11 October 2004, 12770/04 (Presse 276).

49   UNHCR Briefing Notes, 'UNHCR concerned over continued forcible return of potential refugees from Libya', 21 September 2004; Human Rights Watch, 'Libya blocks visit by rights group: torture, political trials, treatment of migrants remain major concerns', 7 December 2004; Amnesty International, 'Urgent Action Update: Eritreans forcibly returned from Libya', 6 September 2004, AI Index: MDE 19/014/2004.

50   UNHCR Briefing Notes, 'Italy: UNHCR Rome granted access at Lampedusa centre, but not in Libya', 8 October 2004.

51   Presidency Conclusions, Edinburgh European Council, 11-12 December 1992 (SN 456/92), Annex 5 Part A: 'Declaration on Principles Governing External Aspects of Migration Policy', paras. IX, XV.

52   Commission of the European Communities, 'On immigration and asylum policies', COM (94) 23 final, 23 February 1994.

53   Austrian Presidency of the European Union, 'Strategy Paper on Immigration and Asylum Policy' (doc. 9809/98 LIMITE CK 4 27 ASIM 170). See also J. Van Selm, 'Immigration and asylum or foreign policy: the EU's approach to migrants and their countries of origin', in S. Lavenex and E. M. Ucarer (eds.), *Migration and the Externalities of European Integration*, 2002, Lanham: Lexington Books, p. 7.

54   As a 2000 COREPER document to the Council stated, 'Developing the JHA external dimension is not an objective in itself. Its primary purpose is to contribute to the establishment of an area of freedom, security and justice. The aim is certainly not to develop a "foreign policy" specific to JHA. Quite the contrary' (Council of the EU, 'European Union priorities and policy objectives for external relations in the field of justice and home affairs', doc. 7653/00, 6 June 2000, p. 5).

55   Dutch Delegation to the Council of the EU, 'Note from the Dutch Delegation: Task Force on Asylum and Migration' (doc. 13344/98 JAI AG 15), 23 November 1998.

56   See Council of the EU, '2158th Council – General Affairs' (Presse 21 Nr: 5455/99), 25 January 1999; COREPER, 'Terms of Reference for the High Level Working Group on Asylum and Migration; preparation of action plans for the most important countries of origin and transit of asylum-seekers and migrants' (doc. 5264/2/99), 22 January 1999.

57   High Level Working Group on Asylum and Migration, 'Report to the European Council in Nice' (doc. 13993/00 (JAI 152 AG76)), 29 November 2000, para. 51.

58   European Parliament, 30 March 2000, *op. cit*., para. F.

59   All member states sent JHA-type officials to the HLWG; Netherlands and Sweden sent teams headed by officials from the ministries of foreign affairs; the UK and Spain sent foreign-affairs ministry staff as part of their team, and other member states sent JHA officials only. (See J. Van Selm, 2002, *op. cit.)*

60   Council of the EU, 'Modification of the Terms of Reference of the High Level Working Group on Asylum and Migration (HLWG)' (doc. 9433/02), 30 May 2002.

61   See Oxfam GB, 2003, *op. cit.*, pp. 43-4.

62   B. Hayes and T. Bunyan, 'Migration, development and the EU security agenda', in H. Mollett (ed.), *Europe in the World: Essays on EU Foreign, Security and Development Policies,* BOND, 2003.

63   R. Pabst, 'The Impact of 11 September 2001 on the Developing Countries and the Implications for EU Development Policy', European Parliament, DG Research Working Paper (doc. DEVE 106 EN 01/2003), 2003.

64   The 2003 European Security Strategy acknowledges that 'our task is to promote a ring of well governed countries to the East of the European Union and on the borders of the Mediterranean with whom we can enjoy close and cooperative relations' (J. Solana, 2003, *op. cit.*, p. 8).

65   See H. Crawley, December 2004, *op. cit*.

66 According to the 2001 census, Muslims comprise seven per cent of the population, and 'others', such as Burghers (the descendants of colonialists), comprise one per cent (UNHCR, Sri Lanka Background Paper, *op. cit.*, p.5).

67 *Ibid.*, p. 5.

68 Interview with UNICEF, Trincomalee.

69 Previous plans for regional devolution that were never implemented include the Bandaranaike–Chelvanayagam Pact of 1957 and the Dudley–Chelvanayagam Pact of 1965 (World Bank, 2003, 'Sri Lanka', *op. cit.*, p. 6).

70 European Union, 'The EU's relations with Sri Lanka', http://europa.eu.int/comm/external_relations/sri_lanka

71 *Ibid.*

72 *Ibid.*

73 ECHO press release, http://europa.eu.int/comm/echo/information/decisions/index_en.cfm.

74 *Ibid.*

75 *Ibid.*

76 European Commission Humanitarian Aid Office (2004), 'Commission allocates EUR 22.5 million for humanitarian aid operations'.

77 *Ibid.*

78 Most of these pledges have been suspended, pending further progress with the peace process. The Conference co-chairs, including Japan, Norway, and the United States, have asked the major donors based in Sri Lanka to identify benchmarks for establishing whether political preconditions are met. Not surprisingly, this has not been an easy exercise so far. While some governments oppose the concept of conditionality, others believe that aid is ineffective in the absence of a commitment to peace.

79 European Commission Delegation to Sri Lanka (2004), press release, 'European Union Election Observation Mission to Sri Lanka', www.dellka.cec.eu.int/en/press_office/press_releases_html/eu_eom_sl.htm (last checked by the author November 2004).

80 Jonathan Goodhand and Charlotte Scawen, 'Oxfam Sri Lanka Relationship Building Programme Review'.

81 Kenneth Bush (1998), 'A Measure of Peace: Peace and Conflict Impact Assessment (PCIA) of Development Projects in Conflict Zones', http://web.idrc.ca/en/ev-28756-201-1-DO_TOPIC.html (last checked by the author November 2004).

Annexes

1 UNHCR, 'Sri Lanka Background Paper', *op. cit.*, p.15.

2 'Agreement on a Ceasefire Between the Government of the Democratic Socialist Republic of Sri Lanka and the Liberation Tigers of Tamil Eelam', www.peaceinsrilanka.org/insidepages/Agreement/agceasefire.asp (last checked November 2004).

3 UNHCR, 'Sri Lanka Background Paper', *op. cit.*, p. 22.

4 *Ibid.*, p. 67.

5 *Ibid.* At the end of 2001, Sri Lankans with refugee status in France, Canada, and the UK numbered 15,774, 13,161, and 11,760, respectively.

6 'The EC and Sri Lanka Co-operation Strategy 2002–2006 and National Indicative Programme for 2003–2005', http://europa.eu.int/comm/external_relations/sri_lanka/csp/index.htm (last checked November 2004).

7 UNHCR, 'Sri Lanka Background Paper', *op. cit.*, p. 67.

8   UNHCR (2004), 'Asylum Levels and Trends: Europe and Non-European Industrialized Countries, 2003', www.unhcr.ch/cgi-bin/texis/vtx/statistics (last checked November 2004).

9   Refugees International (2004), 'Sri Lankan Refugees in India: Hesitant to Return Home', www.refintl.org/content/article/detail/933/ (last checked November 2004).

10 Interview with UNHCR Field Assistant, Killinochchi.

11 Interview with UNHCR, Colombo.

12 Interview with Ministry of Public Security, Law and Order, Colombo.

13 Interview with UNHCR, Colombo.

14 ECHO press release, http://europa.eu.int/comm/echo/information/decisions/index_en.cfm.

15 Interview with EC Delegation staff, Colombo.

16 European Union General Affairs Council High Level Working Group for Asylum and Immigration (1999), 'Action Plan for Sri Lanka', Brussels, pp. 12 and 16.

17 European Delegation to Sri Lanka (2004), 'Sri Lanka signs readmission agreement with European Community', www.dellka.cec.eu.int/en/press_office/press_releases_html/sl_sraw_ec.htm (last checked November 2004).

18 Interview with IOM, Colombo.

19 *Ibid.*

20 Interview with Source Country Information Systems (SCIS), Vienna.

21 *Ibid.*

22 UNHCR (2004), '2003 Global Refugee Trends', www.unhcr.ch/cgi-bin/texis/vtx/statistics (last checked November 2004).

23 UNHCR (2004), '2003 Global Report: United Republic of Tanzania', www.unhcr.ch/cgi-bin/texis/vtx/country?iso=tza (last checked November 2004).

24 *Ibid.*, p. 2.

25 UNHCR (2004), 'UNHCR Activities in Tanzania as of 3 June 2004', Dar es Salaam: UNHCR.

26 *Ibid.*

27 Interview with Tanganyika Christian Refugee Service, Dar es Salaam.

28 The United Republic of Tanzania, Ministry of Home Affairs (2003), 'The National Refugee Policy', Dar es Salaam.

29 The Centre for the Study of Forced Migration, University of Dar es Salaam (2003), 'The Impact of the Presence of Refugees in Northwestern Tanzania', Dar es Salaam: CSFM.

30 Department for International Development (2003) 'DFID Tanzania Country Assistance Plan June 2003 – December 2004', www.dfid.gov.uk/pubs/files/captanzania.pdf (last checked November 2004).

31 *Ibid.*

32 University of Dar es Salaam, 'Impact of Refugees', *op. cit.*, p. 28.

33 *Ibid.*, p. 40.

34 Interview with The Centre for the Study of Forced Migration, University of Dar es Salaam.

35 European Commission (2003) 'EU Relations with Tanzania', http://europa.eu.int/comm/development/body/country/country_home_en.cfm?cid=tz&lng=en&status=new (last checked November 2004).

36 In 2003 ECHO spent €24,000,000 in support of assistance and protection for refugees. In 2004 the budget was reduced to €15,000,000, reflecting a shift in responsibility for €10,000,000 in food aid from ECHO to the AIDCO budget line (interview with ECHO, Dar es Salaam).

37 Inter-Congolese Dialogue (2003), 'The Final Act', www.iss.co.za/AF/profiles/DRCongo/icd/ (last checked November 2004).

38 The Secretary General in August 2004 reported: 'The atmosphere of mistrust among the parties has grown and the lack of political will of some influential players to implement the transitional agenda remains a serious hindrance to progress' (United Nations Security Council, 2004, 'Third Special Report of the Secretary-General on MONUC', *op. cit.*).

39 Figures for August 2004 provided to author by UNOCHA, Kinshasa.

40 UNHCR (2004), 'Refugees by Numbers', www.unhcr.ch (last checked November 2004).

41 United Nations Mission in Democratic Republic of Congo, 'Humanitarian Affairs Section', www.monuc.org/HAS (last checked November 2004).

42 Interview with UNOCHA, Kinshasa.

43 According to UNHCR statistics, 11,523 applications for asylum were lodged by Congolese nationals in Europe in 2002. This is significantly lower than the 8,981 who applied in 2003. Overall, the DRC was the tenth largest source of asylum seekers to the EU in 2003, although in Belgium and France Congolese represent the first and third largest asylum-seeking populations, respectively (UNHCR, 2004, 'Asylum Levels and Trends: Europe and Non-European Industrialized Countries, 2003', www.unhcr.ch, last checked November 2004).

44 *Ibid.*

45 Interview with UNHCR, Kinshasa. These refugees include 124,000 from Angola, 75,000 from Sudan, 20,000 from Uganda, 20,000 from Burundi, 1,000 from Congo-Brazzaville, 1,000 from Rwanda, and several hundred from Central African Republic. An additional 25,000 Rwandans whose status could not be determined during the war live in refugee-like circumstances (US Committee for Refugees, 2004, 'World Refugee Survey 2004: Congo-Kinshasa', www.uscr.org/wrs04/country_updates/africa/congo_kinshasa.html (last checked November 2004).

46 Figures provided by UNOCHA, Kinshasa.

47 Interview with the UK Department for International Development, Kinshasa.

48 Interview with UNOCHA, Kinshasa.

49 As of the mid-term review of the CSP in autumn 2004, there were no specific projects under way directly related to immigration or asylum (interview with DRC Desk Officer, Brussels).

50 EU–DRC, 'Country Strategy Paper', *op. cit.*, p. 36.

Index

African Refugee Convention (1969) 62, 100
arms–trade policies, of the EU 78–9
asylum ii
    and the EU's global reach 14–17
    EU policy makers 30, 92
    internationalised measures driven by home concerns 5
    an issue of concern for the EU 15
    mixed motivations behind internationalisation 3
    new internal and international dimensions 16
    partnerships with third countries 16
    resettlement not a substitute for 48–9
    right to seek, criminalisation of 35
asylum applications, processing outside the EU 59–60
    Hague Programme 66
    UK's New Vision 59
asylum policies, harmonisation of ii, 2
    agenda set by Treaty of Amsterdam 15
    opportunity missed 20–1
    results disappointing 15–16, 21
asylum policy
    focus on 'externalised asylum agenda' iv, 85
    internationalisation of 34
    transfer overseas 4
asylum seekers
    accurate COI information essential 29
    almost impossible to enter Europe legally 35
    caught up in movement of irregular migrants 35
    from Sri Lanka to Europe 95
    interception at EU periphery 2
    movement to Europe influenced by conflict 74
    and refugees, effects of arms trading on 80
    right to have claims examined fairly ii, 30, 88

Belgium, effects of post-WWI policies in the DCR 77
border controls 16
Brussels Conference 2004 3
Bunia after Artemis: non-state agents of protection? 23–4B
    building capacity of the justice system 78

Cap Anamur incident 2, 38
carrier sanctions 38–9
Cartagena Declaration 10
CEAS *see* Common European Asylum System (CEAS)
CFSP *see* EU, Common Foreign and Security Policy (CFSP)
Charter of Fundamental Rights of the European Union 71–2
civil-society organisations 73, 93
COI *see* countries of origin information (COI)
Common European Asylum System (CEAS) 20–1, 61, 88
    minimum standards 30
    second-stage development 30
community–empowerment strategies 11
conflict management 72–4
conflict/underdevelopment/forced migration, links between 74
Congolese refugees
    in refugee camps 99
    resettlement of from Tanzania 51–2B
    vulnerable groups 63
    waiting to return home 61–2
    without a safe haven: women at risk 51–2, 63
Cotonou Agreement 73, 75
countries of origin 2
    root causes of refugee flows v, 70–87, 91–3
countries of origin information (COI) 29–31, 88–9
countries of origin and transit 40, 41
countries of transit 2

Democratic Republic of Congo 4
    Bunia after Artemis: non–state agents of protection? 23–4B
    disarmament not complete 77
    EU action in 77–8
    IDP camps frequently attacked 9
    peoples in the east 24
    profile, 104–8
    risks for returnees 75B
    root causes of conflict and forced displacement in 76–8B
    UN bodies and durable protection 22
development assistance 3
    DRC 77
    EC proposal on 74–5

    not to be contingent on migration-management co-operation 92
    targeted 80
development co-operation 74–5
displacement, durable solutions 11–12
donor fatigue problem 101
DRC *see* Democratic Republic of Congo
durable solutions 60
    access to, Tanzania 62–3
    and displacement 11–12

ECHO (European Community Humanitarian Office) 75, 76
    assistance to refugees in Tanzania 102
    funding use in Sri Lanka 86
    key objectives in the DRC 77–8
effective protection
    an increasingly politicised term 61
    meaning according to UNHCR 60
    possible future restrictive interpretation 67
ENP *see* European Neighbourhood Policy
Eritreans refouled by Malta 39B
EU
    asylum-related policies and bordering regions 16
    Austrian Strategy Paper (1998) 81, 82
    Code of Conduct on Arms Exports 79
    Common Foreign and Security Policy (CFSP) 71, 92
    and conflict prevention 73–4
    cross-pillar policy making 85
    current Country Strategy Paper for the DRC 77, 107
    failure to control arms exports 79
    focus on creating buffer zones 84
    and global standards 17
    major arms suppliers in 79
    needs to address 'root causes' v, 81
    needs a comprehensive approach to migration 70
    needs to be well informed about regional conditions 64–5
    poor quality of co-operation 30
    possible creation of Regional Task Forces 55
    resettlement proposals driven by call for 'orderly entry' 51
    secondary movements into 58
    in Sri Lanka 86
    in Tanzania 102
    through ECHO 66
EU, action in the DRC 77–8
EU, and asylum
    growing influence, global reach 14–17
    proposal to deal with asylum seekers outside EU territory 1
    rise in applications during the 1990s 15
EU, asylum Directives
    do not guarantee international standards 61
    the Procedures Directive 24–30
    Refugee Definition Directive 21–4
EU asylum policy
    a collective concern 14–15
    expert advice essential 17
    and immigration policy 81
    internationalisation of 1
    learning from refugee realities? 3, 17
    need for greater internal consultation 17
    a new way of making 17
    should draw on experiences of ECHO 80, 92
    root causes of refugee flows v, 82
EU Border Police 36
EU Common European Asylum Policy
    internationalised agenda iv, 3
    refugee-protection proposals 2–3
    second-stage draft 2
EU Conflict Prevention Assessment missions 73
    Operation Artemis in the DRC 73
    Proxima, EU Police Mission in Macedonia 73
EU constitution, draft 41
EU, controlling access
    borders, barriers and interception iii, 34–9, 89
EU countries/states
    1990s, perceptions of asylum shopping 15
    and arms supplies 80, 92
    concern to reduce number of asylum seekers on own territory 16
    co-ordinated policies on immigration and asylum 2, 15
    deterrence, not protection, the priority 35
    ensuring effective safeguards 89
    'international' or 'external' policy dimension 2
    must strive to exceed minimum standards and meet commitments 88
need for reliable information on asylum seekers' countries of origin and transit 29
    obligations to asylum seekers 14, 36
    political imperatives responsible for low standards 21
    readmission agreements and international obligations 41–2
    tradition of resettlement on basis of vulnerability and protection needs 56
    unwilling to operate Protected Entry Procedures 90
EU enlarged
    interception methods: divesting responsibility for protection 36–9
EU external policy 71–8
    addressing root causes of conflict in Sri Lanka 85–6
    arms-trade policies 78–9
    coherence or co-operation v–vi, 81–7, 92–3
    conflict management 72–4
    development co-operation 74–5

the High Level Working Group 82–4
human rights 71–2
humanitarian assistance 75–8
impact of v, 70–1, 91–2
necessity for policy coherence 91
EU, harmonisation of asylum policies 2
agenda set by Treaty of Amsterdam 15
results disappointing 15–16
EU ILO Network 37
EU, interception of migrants at sea 38
asylum seekers on island of Lampedusa 38
Cap Anamur problem 2, 38
Eritreans refouled by Malta 39B
Neptune Plan 38
Operation Triton 38
Operation Ulysses 38
Project Deniz 38
EU policy incoherence 79, 80B, 82–4
EU Presidencies (2004–6), and 'Multi-annual Strategic Programme' 16
EU, and readmission agreements 41–2, 90
co-operation on immigration controls with Libya and Syria 42
need for meaningful guarantees from third countries 45, 90
possibility of a EU–China readmission agreement 42
EU, and refugees
danger of developing a two-tier system of rights for 49
provision of safe passage for select few 48
initiatives to ensure more remain in countries of first asylum 58
EU resettlement programme 50–2
EU, securing the co-operation of transit countries 40–5
EURASIL *see* European Union Network of Asylum Practitioners (EURASIL)
European Border Management Agency established 36
European Commission
1994 Communication 81
2004 Communication 60, 64
on access to protection 49
on balance between protection and fight against illegal immigrants 35
development of a Rapid Reaction Mechanism 73, 77
DG JHA 82
and EU external activity 71
European Union Network of Asylum Practitioners (EURASIL) 29–30, 88
focus of aid to Tanzania 102
funding some specific UNHCR projects 64
history of formal co-operation with Sri Lanka 97
JHA priorities currently the priority 82
migration co-operation budget 97
on promotion of human rights and democratisation 72
and protected entry procedures 53
and regional protection programmes 91
relief operations handled by ECHO (humanitarian aid office) 75–6
and Sri Lanka 86
see also ECHO (European Community Humanitarian Office)
European Community 15
European Convention of Human Rights 14
European Council 88
adoption of The Hague Programme 20, 88
call for increased co-ordination 81
and the Charter of Fundamental Rights of the European Union 72
conclusion on durable solutions to the refugee/asylum problem 50
decision-making, individual state veto on asylum legislation removed 17
defines general principles for the CFSP 71
establishment of European Border Management Agency 36
Nice Council (2000) 83
to lift embargo on selling arms to Libya v, 80
European Council, Seville Meeting (2002) 40, 74–5, 82, 84
European Council, Tampere Meeting (1999)
call for closer co-operation between border-control services 36
call for a common EU policy on asylum and immigration 20
EU committed to respecting right to asylum 35, 88
EU seeking more international approach to immigration and asylum 16
European Council, Thessaloniki Meeting (2003) 41, 60
European Court of Justice 17
European Neighbourhood Policy: focus on transit countries iii, 43–4
refugee-protection capacities, third countries 45, 90
European Parliament
concluded that Action Plans (from HLWG) made no real contributions 83
opposed to UK's New Vision protection regime 59
role in asylum policy making to increase from 2005 21
to continue dialogue with stakeholder groups 88
to have more say in decision making on asylum matters 17
European Union Network of Asylum Practitioners (EURASIL) 29–30
EU's Special Envoy for the Great Lakes Region 78
extra-territorial processing *see* asylum applications, processing outside the EU

Index 127

forced displacement
- and conflict, addressing root causes of, Sri Lanka 85–6B
- and conflict, root causes of, DRC 76–8B
- facts and figures 95, 99–100, 105
- size of problem 8–9

gender-based violence 9
- Lugufu camps I and II 63
- *see also* women

gender-specific persecution, recognised in the Refugee Definition Directive 22
Global Commission on Internal Migration (GCIM) 85
global refugee population 8

Hague Programme 20, 30, 64, 66, 88
High Level Working Group 65, 82–4, 87, 92, 97
HLWG *see* High Level Working Group
human rights
- and EU external policy 71–2
- of refugees and displaced people 10

Human Rights Watch 9, 14
human-rights violations
- communication of 31
- facilitated by arms transfers 79
- and refugee movements 71
- and violent conflict 72

humanitarian assistance 3, 75–8
- provision of by EU 75–6, 77–8
- root causes of conflict and displacement in the DRC 76–8B

humanitarian relief in the DRC 77

IDP camps
- Bunia 24
- frequently attacked, in DRC 9

IDPs *see* internally displaced people
illegal immigration
- call for a negative migration conditionality 40
- interception measures 36, 37
- need for EU to monitor third countries 41
- root causes (Seville Meeting) 82
- to have higher priority in EU policy 30

ILOs *see* immigration liaison officers (ILOs)
immigration, and the state 15
immigration liaison officers (ILOs) 37
India, Sri Lankan refugees in 95–6
information, accurate, need for 29–30
integration, local, an alternative to 'warehousing' of refugees 11
interception measures
- aimed at illegal immigrants, barrier for asylum seekers 37
- at Prague Airport 37B
- at sea 38
- defined 36
- divesting responsibility for protection 36–9
- presented as tools in fight against illegal immigration 36

internally displaced people 8, 10, 27
- in refugee camps 9, 24, 106–7
- in Sri Lanka 96

International Arms Trade Treaty 79, 92
International Centre for Migration Policy Development (ICMPD) 97
International Conferences on Africa (ICARA) 65
International Criminal Court, Ituri district 78
international law, and state responsibilities for protection needs 36
International Organisation for Migration (IOM) 10, 97
international organisations, work of 48–9
international refugee law, and UK actions at Prague Airport 37
Ituri, DRC 105
- massacre, rape, and cannibalism reported 23
- official investigation by International Criminal Court 78
- Operation Artemis 107

Kosovo, UNMIK forces in 22
Kurdish Autonomous Area (KAA), UK Court of Appeal ruling 22

Least Developed Countries (LDCs), hosting refugee populations 8
lessons from Lugufu: what makes protection effective? 61–3B
Libya v, 80, 80B
Lomé IV Convention, and Cotonou Agreement 75
Lusaka Accord 105

Malta, Eritreans forcibly deported from 39B
Mediterranean Sea, interception policies of EU member states in 38
migration, forced
- addressing root causes of 74
- and violent conflict 72

migration, irregular, and political extremism 34
migration management iii
- co-operation for in the DRC 107
- concerns 3, 44, 54, 89, 90
- countries identified for intensive EU co-operation on 40
- initiatives should not undermine/contradict promotion of human rights 80
- migration-management impact assumption questionable 65–6
- needs co-operation of countries of origin and transit 40

North Africa a focus for co-operation agreements 44
  prospect of further geo-politicisation of refugee assistance 66
  seen as necessary and inevitable by EU states 34
  should not dominate/dictate EU relationships with third countries 44
migration-management clauses, integration into EU external agreements 3

Nairobi Protocol 79
the Netherlands 66
NGOs 48–9
  many excluded from consultation process 21
  working to improve refugee protection 11
non-refoulement principle 9, 89
  applies when asylum seekers present for entry 35
  a central principle of international law 39
  could be regularly breached through carrier sanctions 38–9
  must be present in readmission or migration-management agreements 44
  threatened by safe countries clauses 25
non-state agents of protection ii
  Bunia after Artemis 23–4B
  cannot guarantee to fulfil duties of a state 30
  a worrying idea 22
North Africa, and migration-management co-operation agreements 44

Operation Artemis ii, 23, 73, 107
orderly entry 60
  doubts about true motivations 65
  new approaches to 48–56, 90
Organization for Security and Co-operation in Europe (OSCE) 79
Oxfam, work in Sri Lanka 98
Oxfam, work in the DRC 107–8
Oxfam, work in Tanzania 102–3

Pakistan 11
Prague Airport: UK immigration officers targeting asylum seekers 37
Procedures Directive 24–30
  binding common list of safe countries of origin ii, 25
  need for accurate information 29–30
  No war, no peace in Sri Lanka 26–8B
  'safe countries' clauses, threats in 24–5
  UNHCR concern with draft 24
protected entry procedures 48, 52–4

Rapid Reaction Mechanism 73, 77
  funded peace-building initiatives in Sri Lanka 86
readmission agreements 41–2, 89, 90
recommendations, summary of 88–93
refugee
  defined in Refugee Convention 71
  defined in Refugee Definition Directive 21–2
  recognition as enables states to offer protection 71
  UN definition 9–10
refugee camps
  basic security often lacking 9
  refugees often denied basic rights 8
Refugee Convention (1951) 14, 100
  Article 33, concerning non-refoulement 9
  freedom of movement for refugees within the host country 62
  not signed by Libya or Syria 42
  principle of international solidarity, 2001 declaration 10
  rights of refugees to seek asylum and to be protected 1
Refugee Definition Directive 21–4
refugee flows, root causes of 70–87
refugee protection 1–3
  a global responsibility 5
  rights to not always met in prosperous stable countries 1
  states have a primary protection responsibility 10
  whose responsibility? 10–11
refugee realities ii
  detailed knowledge held by many stakeholders vi, 3
  learning from 17
refugee realities, view from the ground 8–12
  ending displacement, durable solutions 11–12
  forced displacement 8–9
  global standards to protect refugees 9–10
  who is responsible for protecting refugees? 10–11
refugee-hosting countries
  arms trading can negatively affect development efforts 78
  responsible for realisation of refugees' full rights within available resources 91
  see also Tanzania
refugees
  Angolan, repatriation from DRC planned 106
  DRC home to a large number 105–6
  global standards for protection 9–10
  host countries should undertake realisation of full rights 67
  majority hosted in developing countries 60
  many organisations work with daily 10
  may be forced to move from first country of asylum through lack of protection 58
  respect for dignity of must be paramount at all times 12
  in Sri Lanka 96

Sri Lankan, in India 95–6
Sudanese repatriation plans on hold 106
vulnerable, waiting for resettlement missions 55–6
'warehoused' in camps in forced dependency 8, 100
see also Congolese refugees
region of origin, enhancing protection or exporting asylum iv, 58–67
    recent developments: processing centres back on the agenda 66–7
    regional protection programmes 60–3
    tool boxes and action plans 64–5
    unanswered questions 65–6
region of origin, new approaches to orderly entry 48–56, 90
    moves towards an EU resettlement programme 50–2
    protected entry procedures 52–4
    resettlement, not a substitute for asylum 48–9
regional governments, dialogue with EU, refugee protection and host community welfare paramount 67, 91
regional protection areas (RPAs) iv, 59
regional protection programmes 3
    back on the agenda 66–7
    bargaining counter in negotiating partnership agreements 66
    disturbing possible future use of 67
    include humanitarian assistance and development elements 3
    potential to make positive impacts 65
    should comprise well-targeted, well-resourced long-term initiatives 67, 91
    should not be used as a bargaining counter 67, 90
    source of finances would influence direction of programmes 65
    strengthening the protection capacity of refugees' region of origin 60–3
    strengthening protection capacity of some African countries 64
    tool box activities 64
regions of origin iv
    enhancing protection or exporting asylum 91
    host communities and EU improvement of local infrastructure 65
    increasing the EU presence in 55–6
    protection capacity to be increased 2
reintegration assistance for ex-combatants in DRC 77
repatriation
    most desirable option 11
    must mean 'voluntary return in safety and dignity' 11
resettlement 2
    European tradition of based on vulnerability and need 90
    not a substitute for asylum 48–9
    of refugees to a third country 11, 96
    resourcing in Tanzania 52
    tool for international protection 56, 90
resettlement schemes 48
root causes v–vi, 81, 83
    coherence and co-operation needed 85, 92
    of conflict and forced displacement, Sri Lanka 85–6B
    of forced displacement and conflict, DRC 76–8B
    of forced migration 74
    of illegal immigration 82
    minimal attention to by EU now 82
    of refugee flows 70–87
    should be explicitly mapped by the EU 92
RPAs *see* regional protection areas (RPAs)
RPPs *see* regional protection programmes
Rwandan genocide 73

'safe countries', Procedures Directive 24–6
safe countries of origin 24–5
    no EU lists should be drawn up 30
    not all EU states hold a list of 25
safe third-country provisions 25
security, in Bunia 24
security concerns, increased 84, 92
self-sufficiency, and freedom, dignity of 63
sexual violence
    resettlement of survivors 51–2
    to women and children 9
Somali Bantu refugees, resettlement in USA from Kenya 11
Srebrenica (1995), massacre in UN Safe Area 22
Sri Lanka 4
    addressing root causes of conflict and forced displacement 85–6B
    aftermath of the tsunami 27
    cultural attitudes discourage direct dialogue 26
    human-rights reports show abuses continuing 26
    Indian Peace Keeping Force 85
    local leaders afraid to challenge LTTE in public 27
    LTTE targets all who oppose the movement 26
    Muslim community resisted concept of Tamil homeland 85
    negotiation of a EU readmission agreement premature iii
    no war, no peace in 26–8B
    perceived Tamil dominance led to Sinhalese backlash 85
    problems faced by female ex-cadres 27–8
    protected entry procedures in practice: the Swiss Embassy 54B
    readmission agreements premature 42B
    still at risk: children, deserters, and dissidents 27–8
    UNHCR mandate covers refugees and IDPs 10
Sri Lanka profile 94–8
    EU in Sri Lanka 97
    forced displacement: facts and figures 95

Oxfam's work in Sri Lanka 98
political background 94–5
refugees in Sri Lanka 96
Sri Lankan refugees in India 95–6
Sri Lankan IDPs 27, 96
Sri Lankan government, immigration legislation 96
Stability Pact for South-Eastern Europe 73
Switzerland
offers a protected entry programme for Sri Lankans iv, 54B

Tanzania 4, 11
Congolese refugees, returning home not an option for most 63
current focus on repatriating Burundian refugees 63
party to both UN and African Refugee Conventions 62
policy of repatriation for all refugees 62–3
problems of urban refugees 9
resettlement of Congolese iv, 51–2B
see also Lessons from Lugufu: what makes protection effective?
Tanzania profile 99–103
the EU in Tanzania 102
forced displacement: facts and figures 99–100
limitations to refugee-hosting capacity 101–2
new National Refugee Policy 101
Oxfam's work in Tanzania 102–3
political background: Tanzania's refugee policy 100–1
refugees in Tanzania: new arrivals from the DRC 100
TPCs *see* transit processing centres (TPCs)
transit countries, securing co-operation of iii, 40–5, 89–90
European neighbourhood policy 43–4, 89
focus on North Africa 44
partnerships for immigration control, at what cost 40–1
readmission agreements: returns without safeguards 41–2
transit processing centres (TPCs) 2, 59, 60, 66–7, 91
Treaty of Amsterdam (1997)
affected asylum policy 15
annexed declaration, on establishing consultation with UNHCR 17
reaffirms EU's founding principles 71
tsunami disaster, Sri Lanka 27
European Commission, humanitarian relief 86
Oxfam's emergency and rehabilitation work 98

UK
House of Lords decision on targeting of asylum seekers at Prague Airport 37
New Vision, based on TPCs and RPAs 59, 60
UN, Security Council Resolution authorising intervention in Bunia 23

UN Convention Relating to the Status of Refugees *see* Refugee Convention (1951)
UN Mission in DRC (MONUC) 23
UN Programme of Action on Small Arms and Light Weapons 79
UN Secretary General
Global Commission on Internal Migration (GCIM) 85
High Level Panel on Threats, Challenges and Change 73
UN Security Council
human-rights violations justify Chapter VII action 73
primary responsibility for maintaining international peace and security 73
UNHCR 9, 48–9
Agenda for Protection 35, 82, 87, 92
called for draft Procedures Directive (EU) to be taken off the table 24
cases of actual refoulement on Lake Tanganyika 62
established district-level protection networks in Sri Lanka 96
facilitating refugee returns in DRC 106
mandate may sometimes cover IDPs 10
on meaning of effective protection 60
monitors returning Sri Lankan refugees from India 96
opts now for 'quality' protection 61
principle of non-refoulement 35, 37
projects to strengthen asylum systems in North Africa 44
resettlement and asylum, distinct and separate possibilities 49
resettlement referrals in Tanzania 51, 52
state assistance often channelled through 10
supported by ECHO 75
supports refugees in Sri Lanka while pursuing third-country resettlement 96
UNHCR–Sri Lanka, and returns of Sri Lankan refugees from India 96
UNICEF 27, 106
urban refugees 9
USA
large-scale resettlements of Somali Bantu refugees 11
regularly carries out resettlement 49

women
and children, subject to sexual violence 9, 63
expoited and abused by MONUC troops 23
problem of ex–cadres in Sri Lanka 27–8
violence against widespread in armed environments 79
World Food Programme (WFP) 10, 106
funding shortages led to supply problems at Lugufu camps 62

Zimbabwe, imposition of visa restrictions on all Zimbabweans 52